UNDE

Understanding The Gospel

SINCLAIR B FERGUSON

KINGSWAY PUBLICATIONS
EASTBOURNE

First published 1989

Front cover design by Vic Mitchell

British Cataloguing in Publication Data

Ferguson, Sinclair, B
Understanding the Gospel
1. Bible. N.T. Mark. Critical studies
I. Title
226'.306

ISBN 0-86065-499-0

Production and printing in Great Britain for
KINGSWAY PUBLICATIONS LTD
1 St Anne's Road, Eastbourne, E Sussex BN21 3UN by
Nuprint Ltd, 30b Station Road, Harpenden, Herts AL5 4SE

For
ANNE FLAVELLE
In Memory of
ALAN
who followed Jesus Christ
and encouraged others
to come with him

Contents

Preface

Jesus Christ is the heart of the Christian faith and the centre of the Christian life. If we want to learn about him, we must read one of the Gospels. If we want to become his disciples, we must study one of the Gospels to learn what discipleship means. If we wish to tell others about what he has done, we must tell them what is in one of the Gospels.

Yet many of us are not really familiar with the Jesus of the Gospels. *Understanding the Gospel* is an explanation of the earliest of the four, and is specifically written to increase our familiarity with him. Its origin lies in a series of studies written for the weekly newspaper *The Christian Herald* during 1985 and the first half of 1986. Following the encouragement of Christopher Catherwood I have entirely rewritten and expanded them. 'Living' for so many hours in the Gospel of Mark has been an enriching experience for me, as I have followed Jesus from place to place, from miracle to miracle, from controversy to controversy, and from the River Jordan (where Mark's Gospel begins) to the Garden Tomb. It has been challenging to devote so much time to thinking about him, and has left me with a fresh sense of who Jesus really is and what he is really like. I hope that some echo of that will be heard in these pages.

Understanding the Gospel is intended to provide an introduction to Jesus and to Christian faith and life. Many people who begin to show an interest in Christian teaching wonder where to begin. I hope this will prove to be an ideal starting place.

It has also been written with a view to Bible study on a regular basis. It can be used individually or for group study. I also hope that many families will find it suitable and helpful for using in family devotions.

Like mothers with children, authors discover that each book they 'bring to birth' has its own special associations and memories. In this connection I would like to thank Christopher Catherwood for his encouragement to produce *Understanding the Gospel*, and especially my wife, Dorothy, and our children for coping with this unplanned 'addition' to the family.

The dedication of this book marks what was, for me, a very special relationship. Dr Alan Flavelle, Minister of Lowe Memorial Church, Finaghy, Belfast, was old enough to have been my own father, spiritually. He was an elder brother to me in the family of God, a pastor, a wise counsellor, a special encourager and a greatly loved friend. His vibrant life demonstrated the presence, power and relevance of the risen Christ. After a long and heroic struggle against severe illness, he was called into Christ's presence in the week in which these pages were completed. The dedication of *Understanding the Gospel* is but a fragmentary indication of my gratitude and profound admiration for what Christ made him.

SINCLAIR B FERGUSON

I

The Gospel According to Mark

When John Mark wrote out his 'good news' about Jesus two thousand years ago, his Gospel was a completely new kind of book. No one had ever written one before. In fact, no one would have known what a Gospel was!

Of course, books about great men and the records of their lives had been composed. What made the Gospel of Mark unique was this: it was not written merely as the memoir of Jesus as a great man, not even of the greatest man who had ever lived. Rather, it was meant to persuade its readers that Jesus was the Son of God. Mark says as much in the first words of his book: 'The beginning of the gospel about Jesus Christ, the Son of God.'

This theme—the identity of Jesus of Nazareth—is one which reappears in the course of the story of his life and work. Mark records how, later, Jesus himself raises the question: 'Who do people say I am?' (Mk 8:27). At the climax of the Gospel, the same question appears. This time it is found on the lips of the high priest: 'Are you the Christ, the Son of the Blessed One?' (Mk 14:61). It is the central question in the entire book. It keeps appearing, in different ways, to remind us that this is the question we are being invited to ask, and to answer, for ourselves.

Who is Jesus of Nazareth? What is the good news (gospel) about him?

We all have our own answer to that question. This book presents us with Mark's answer. It is full of important information which will help us to understand what Jesus said and did, what his life was really like, and who he claimed to be. It is the earliest reliable record we have about him. For that reason, understanding Mark's Gospel is a major step in coming to know, understand and believe in Jesus himself.

The author of the Gospel

Although we call this book 'Mark's Gospel', it was actually written anonymously. But there is an unbroken tradition in the Christian church, dating back to the second century, that it was indeed written by John Mark.

Around the year AD 140, Papias, who was the bishop of the church at Hierapolis, recorded something he had heard from an older contemporary:

> The elder said this also: "Mark, having become the interpreter of Peter, wrote down accurately whatever he remembered of the things said and done by the Lord, but not however in order."

Within another forty years, two further testimonies tell the same story. An anonymous preface to the Gospel of Mark, written sometime after AD 160, records:

> Mark...who is called "stump-fingered", because he had rather small fingers in comparison with the stature of his body. He was the interpreter of Peter. After the death of Peter himself he wrote down this same gospel in the region of Italy.

A similar testimony is found among the writings of a leading early Christian writer, Irenaeus of Lyons:

> After the death of (Peter and Paul) Mark, the disciple of Peter, also transmitted to us in writing the things preached by Peter.

These statements tell us a number of things about this Gospel. It was written by John Mark who was the friend and disciple of Simon Peter. In fact, the Gospel Mark wrote was in a sense Peter's; Irenaeus even suggests that Mark's Gospel contains the kind of account of Jesus which Simon Peter himself used to give in his preaching.

You will notice this as you read through the Gospel. Parts of it breathe the air of an eye-witness account, others even express Peter's own personality. In Mark's Gospel, everything seems to happen 'immediately' or 'without delay'. That sounds just like Simon Peter!

In this connection, it is interesting to notice the similarity between the sermon Peter preached to the household of Cornelius, and the structure of Mark's Gospel.

> This is the message God sent to the people of Israel, telling the good news of peace through Jesus Christ, who is Lord of all. You know what has happened throughout Judea, beginning in Galilee after the baptism that John preached—how God anointed Jesus of Nazareth with the Holy Spirit and power, and how he went around doing good and healing all who were under the power of the devil, because God was with him.
>
> We are witnesses of everything he did in the country of the Jews and in Jerusalem. They killed him by hanging him on a tree, but God raised him from the dead on the third day and caused him to be seen. He was not seen by all the people, but by witnesses whom God had already chosen—by us who ate and drank with him after he rose from the dead. He commanded us to preach to the people and to testify that he is the one whom God has appointed as judge of the living and the dead. All the prophets testify about him that everyone who believes in him receives forgiveness of sins through his name.
>
> (Acts 10:36–43)

Like the Gospel, the sermon begins with the baptism by John in Jordan, the anointing of Jesus with the Spirit, and the ministry of Jesus beginning in Galilee and ending in Jerusalem. It then records the eye-witness account of what Jesus did in Jerusalem, his crucifixion and resurrection. The Gospel follows the outline of Peter's sermon very closely. Both convey the sense of commitment to Jesus Christ which we know Peter had, and which Mark himself was eventually to show.

John who?

We know relatively little about John Mark (to give him his full name). It is almost certain that he was a native of Jerusalem. His mother, Mary, owned a house there large enough for many Christians to gather in it for prayer (Acts 12:12). The family were closely related to Barnabas, one of the leading early Christians, and also a man of considerable wealth (Acts 4:36–37).

It has been suggested that Mark actually identifies himself in the course of writing his Gospel. Two anonymous figures appear towards the end of the narrative. Mark 14:14 refers to a householder in Jerusalem in whose home the disciples and Jesus celebrated the Passover. Mark 14:51 refers to a young man who fled naked from the scene of Jesus' arrest. It is certainly not impossible that these are references to Mark—rather like the appearance of an artist in some minor role in a scene he had painted himself. More important, and certain, is the fact that Mark joined the mission of Paul and Barnabas (Acts 12:25). Later, however, he left and returned to Jerusalem under something of a cloud. When Barnabas suggested that Mark should accompany them again, Paul refused. So considerable was the difference over him that Paul and Barnabas thereafter engaged on separate missions.

It is encouraging to discover that Mark reappears in the New Testament in three of Paul's letters. In Colossians 4:10, Paul writes: 'My fellow-prisoner Aristarchus sends you his greetings, as does Mark, the cousin of Barnabas. (You have received instructions about him; if he comes to you, welcome him.)' Obviously Paul and Mark were united again, the past had been forgiven, and Paul was making certain that none of the churches belittled Mark because of what had happened.

In Philemon verse 24, Paul mentions Mark as one of his 'fellow-workers'.

In Paul's last recorded letter, he urged Timothy: 'Get Mark and bring him with you, because he is helpful to me in my ministry' (2 Tim 4:11). No more eloquent testimony to John Mark's value as a Christian could be expected.

Later in the New Testament records, we find Mark alongside Simon Peter as his 'son' in the faith (1 Pet 5:13). Peter and his little group of fellow-workers are in 'Babylon' at this time, probably a reference to Rome. If this is so, it confirms the early traditions in the Christian church that Mark originally wrote the Gospel in Italy and for the use of the church at Rome.

As you read through the Gospel, this background may bring its contents to life, from time to time. Here is someone writing about Jesus who was probably on the fringes of the early disciple band; his relatives included those who had known him; his friends and perhaps even his parents were those who had known him well. Here is a man who has had first-hand knowledge of the Apostles Peter and Paul. Not only so, but he has experienced failure as well as success in the service of Christ. Perhaps it was this that first drew him so close to Peter. It was certainly this that would have helped him to understand how Peter must sometimes have felt during the ministry of Jesus. Now Mark is in Rome and writing for a church which the Roman Emperor is persecuting. Paul has been martyred and Peter too; the infant church is like a ship tossed on the waves of an uncontrollable storm as it had been during Jesus' ministry (Mk 4:35–41). Will it survive? Where will it find strength? This Gospel provides the answers to these questions—and not only for the early church—for the church today as well. It was good news for the first century, it is good news for our own too!

2

The Pattern of Mark's Gospel

Mark's Gospel develops the story of Jesus' ministry in a very straightforward and simple way.

Introduction

1:1–13. Jesus' ministry is set in the context of the ministry of his forerunner, John the Baptist.

Ministry in Galilee

1:14–6:13. Jesus' early public ministry in Galilee. Already in this section, Mark introduces us to the beginnings of the conflict between the religious leaders and Jesus which we shall see runs through the whole of the Gospel.

Jesus is described as the Lord of men and nature, and teaches some of the great principles which govern life in his kingdom. This section includes the rejection he experienced in his home town of Nazareth, and his sending out of his disciples to preach and teach the message he had brought concerning the kingdom of God.

Withdrawn from conflict

6:14–8:30. A period of withdrawal which comes to a climax with Simon Peter confessing his faith in Jesus as the promised Messiah of God.

Towards Jerusalem

8:31–10:52. Jesus explains that he is a suffering Messiah, and will die in Jerusalem. The section ends with Jesus passing through Jericho on his way to Jerusalem for the last time in his life.

The conflict heightens

11:1–13:37. Jesus ministers in Jerusalem, preaching and teaching in a context in which the opposition and scheming of the religious leaders grows almost daily, leading to its climax.

The Passion

14:1–15:47. Jesus spends his last hours with his disciples before he is betrayed by one of them and arrested, tried by Jewish and Roman leaders alike. In a 'rigged' trial his opponents cannot produce evidence from their witnesses sufficient to condemn him. But he is condemned nevertheless, taken out and executed by crucifixion. He is buried in a borrowed tomb in front of which a large gravestone is rolled.

The Resurrection

16:1–end. The Gospel comes to an end with the story of the Resurrection of Jesus. Jesus is risen and is alive for evermore!

3
In The Beginning
Mark 1:1–8

How did the gospel begin? Each of the four Gospels gives us a slightly different perspective on that question. Matthew traces the story back through the family tree of Jesus to the Patriarch Abraham, to whom God had given his wonderful promises (Mt 1:1–17).

Luke traces it even further back. He wanted to emphasise the universal appeal of Jesus, and so he set his life and ministry in the context of the whole of human history, from the beginning in Adam and Eve (Lk 3:21–37).

In a sense, John traces the gospel back even further. He calls Jesus 'the Word' of God, and tells us that his origin lies in eternity. He was with God in the beginning (Jn 1:1–14).

Mark begins his Gospel by telling us two simple things. First, the gospel is about Jesus Christ. It is not good advice about how to live, but good news about a person. Then secondly, Mark sets the scene for Jesus by telling us about John the Baptist and the significance of his life and ministry.

Scripture fulfilled

In Malachi 3:1, God had promised that he would send a messenger to the people before the coming of his Messiah, whose task would be to prepare the way. Isaiah 40:3 gave a further description of this messenger. He would be a 'voice in the desert'. His message would be: 'Prepare for the coming of the Lord.'

The coming of Jesus was not an afterthought on God's part. It was something for which he had planned and prepared during the long years of the Old Testament. Now the time had come for God to work. He sent John as the messenger he had promised so long before. After centuries of silence, many recognised that God was speaking to his people once again. Now he was saying something new: God was about to speak for the last time.

Mark runs together two quotations here. He introduces them with the words: 'It is written in Isaiah the prophet.' Yet it is only the second quotation which comes from Isaiah. Why should they both have the same introduction? Did Mark make a mistake? Could it be that he didn't know his Bible very well? Is this—right at the beginning of the earliest Gospel—an indication that it is far from being an error-free description of Jesus?

It stretches credibility to think that Mark would make such an elementary mistake. Perhaps he was quoting these words from an already existing summary of Old Testament texts which had been gathered together to bear witness to Jesus. The probable explanation is that it is only when Malachi 3:1 is quoted alongside the passage from Isaiah that the full significance of what Isaiah says is clear. The voice which cries out in the desert is actually the herald who immediately precedes his Master's visitation. Together the two passages explain John's significance and his relationship to Jesus. They indicate not only that the Lord's way was to be prepared, but that he was coming very soon.

Preaching repentance

The burden of John's preaching was repentance (v 4). He exposed his hearers' sins and called on them to turn from them, washing them away symbolically in the River Jordan by being baptised. Only in this way would they enjoy forgiveness and a new life.

John was the last of the Old Testament prophets. He made a tremendous impression on his contemporaries. Huge numbers came to hear him speak. There was what we would call a revival. People even came from Jerusalem to hear him. Think of going to the Yorkshire Dales from London because you had heard there was a man there who preached as though he really knew God and men's hearts too! Even some of those who attended Jerusalem's temple services were noticed among the listeners.

Everything about John told people he was a prophet. He was in the mould of Elijah. His clothing was 'desert-wear'; his diet was desert food. He stood out from his contemporaries as clearly and recognisably as his great predecessor (see 2 Kings 1:8).

John's message was also similar to Elijah's. The people had broken the covenant with God. They were under his judgement. Only by turning away from their sins and turning back to the Lord and his ways would they be ready when the long-promised Messiah came.

Pointing to Jesus

In the Old Testament, the task of the prophet was twofold. He spoke God's word about the present, and he shared God's word about the future. We find John doing both of these things. He forth-told and fore-told the message of the Lord. He explained to the people the significance of the Messiah's coming: he would be more powerful than John. So much greater would his dignity be that John was scarcely worthy to tie the thongs of his sandals (v 7). John also prophesied what this Messiah would do. In contrast with John's baptism with water, the One who came after him would baptise people with the Spirit of God himself.

John preached that the turning point of human history was about to take place. The Messiah was about to come. Only one adequate response was open to the people: repentance.

The style and content of John's ministry have a great deal to teach us today. His preaching was Spirit-directed in a special way. Like the Spirit, he did not seek glory for himself (see John 16:13–14). Instead he pointed people to Jesus. There is no clearer mark that we are filled with the Spirit of God. For the fullness of the Spirit does not primarily show itself in signs and wonders, but in the way we say (with John): '[Christ] must become greater; I must become less' (Jn 3:30).

Have you ever said that?

4

The Messiah

Mark 1:9–13

One of the outstanding features of Mark's Gospel is its fast-moving style. He conveys a sense of constant activity in several interesting ways. For example, Mark constructs many of his sentences simply by joining one statement to another by the use of 'and'. He frequently uses the Greek word 'immediately'. In these simple ways he makes us feel the energy of the events he is describing.

He produces the same effect by describing very briefly what other Gospel writers spend a good deal of time on. The baptism and temptation of Jesus illustrate this. Matthew and Luke describe them in considerable detail (see Matthew 4 and Luke 4), while Mark devotes only a handful of verses to this strategic event in Jesus' life.

This does not mean that Mark wanted to play down these events. In fact, the brevity of his description underlines the starkness of what took place: Jesus, the Saviour, the Son of God, stood with sinners in the River Jordan and was baptised by John. Jesus, the Lord of Creation (as Mark will later explain), went hungry and thirsty in the wilderness and was tempted by the Devil. Mark did not feel that the contrast between Jesus' personal identity and

Jesus' experience as Saviour needed to be underlined. It was enough simply to state the facts: he was the Son of God, yet he entered into the arena of flesh and blood, shared his life with sinful men and women, and experienced to the full the fiercest of onslaughts from the Tempter.

Mark identifies three elements in these verses.

Inauguration

The baptism of Jesus marked his public inauguration as the Messiah. He came into the world to be the Saviour of sinners. Now, for the first time, he engages in an activity which shows this. He has not come in pomp and circumstance to lord it over men; but in lowliness and humility, to save them. Here already he indicates how he will become our Saviour: by standing in the River whose waters had washed away the sins of the penitent Jews, and allowing that water, polluted by those sins, to be poured over his perfect being.

Unlike the other Gospel writers, it did not serve Mark's purposes to tell his readers how John actually argued with Jesus about his being baptised. John knew that Jesus did not need to be baptised as a symbol of repentance—he had no sins from which he needed to repent. He was the spotless Lamb of God, who needed no offer of forgiveness. But Mark allows the inherent 'contradiction' to stand, because it leads us directly to the heart of Jesus' ministry. His baptism inaugurates him publicly into his role of the priest who bears away the sins of men in order to bring them forgiveness and salvation.

Jesus' water baptism inaugurated him into a ministry which reached its fulfilment later in his baptism in blood upon the cross (see Luke 12:50). What we have here is Jesus' public acknowledgement that he had come to stand where sinners should stand, receive what they should deserve, and in return give to them his gift of grace and fellowship with God.

Identification

As Jesus was coming out of the water, he saw heaven being torn open and the Spirit descending on him like a dove. It was an assurance to him of God's approval of his actions. Furthermore, now that he had publicly committed himself to his task of salvation, he was being 'sealed' by the Holy Spirit (Jn 6:27).

The *visual* part of God's seal came in the presence of the dove-Spirit. It is a reminder of the way in which God's judgement came to an end when the dove which Noah sent from the ark found a place to rest. It symbolises the beginning of God's new creation. It was as though he was saying: Jesus is the One in whom I will begin again.

But there was also a *verbal* part to God's seal of approval on Jesus. A voice spoke from heaven to identify him. It explained Jesus' identity by means of the Old Testament promises. Jesus is God's beloved Son; the One whom God loves; Jesus is the One with whom the Father is well pleased. Three Old Testament passages are used here. There is an echo of the voice which Abraham heard when he was challenged to sacrifice his only, much-loved son (Gen 22:2); then of the proclamation of the Son as King (Ps 2:7); lastly there is an echo of the words which introduce the Suffering Servant (Is 42:1).

The voice from heaven bears witness to Jesus' identity. He is the Son of God, the King in God's kingdom; he is much-loved and enjoys a unique relationship with his Father. He is also the One who has come to suffer for the sins of the people, the servant who would be wounded, bruised and chastised for others (Is 53:4–6).

The whole of Jesus' own understanding of his task and ministry is summarised in these three statements.

Temptation

Mark's record now takes an unexpected turn. The Spirit of God has just descended on Jesus; now the same Spirit sends him out into the desert to face an onslaught of temptation from the hands of the Devil. And why should Mark (alone) specifically mention that Jesus was with 'wild animals' (v 13)?

Jesus Christ came to be what Paul called the last Adam and the second man (1 Cor 15:45, 47). He came to undo what Adam had done by his sin and fall. But if he were to reverse what Adam had done, he needed to enter into the world not as Adam found it but as Adam had left it. So when he was tempted, he was not in a garden, like Adam. He was not, like Adam, surrounded by the animals over which he exercised dominion (Gen 1:28). He was in a desert, surrounded by wild beasts. It was in a fallen, broken, sinful, disintegrating world that Jesus faced temptation and the powers of darkness, in order to win for his people a way back to the Tree of Life.

5

The Reign of God

Mark 1:14–20

The stage has now been set by Mark for the ministry of Jesus. John has been the herald of his coming. His Father and his Spirit had also heralded his identity as the long-promised Messiah. He had faced his inaugural conflict with the kingdom of darkness. Now John the Baptist had been imprisoned. It was time for Jesus to begin his ministry in word and action. These verses record a summary of the message Jesus preached, and the impact he made upon people as he summoned them to respond to it.

The message

Jesus' message is outlined in verses 14–15. It is, first of all, 'good news'. Interestingly, the passage which Mark had cited from Isaiah 40 (in verse 3) had also spoken about the proclamation of good news. In fact the subject matter was the same: 'See, the Sovereign Lord comes with power, and his arm rules for him' (Is 40:9–10). Isaiah had spoken about the 'gospel' of the reign of God in a world of darkness and disintegration. Now Jesus was saying that the message which Isaiah had prophesied was being fulfilled: 'The kingdom of God is near' (v 15).

The kingdom

What did Jesus mean? We tend to associate a kingdom with a geographical area over which a monarch reigns. But in Scripture 'the kingdom of God' describes an activity: God's reign over his people and his world. That rule was exercised wherever God was present. The Old Testament revelation had led people to believe that one day God would establish that reign personally. This was the 'good news' which Isaiah had brought. Jesus' words meant: the time has come; God's reign is beginning to be seen. But how? In Jesus himself. That was the meaning of the word from Psalm 2 spoken at his baptism. God was publicly installing his Son as King in his kingdom. From now on Jesus would speak and act publicly with authority and majesty.

The stories which follow are meant to illustrate the reign of God, now present among men in Jesus himself. He calls men into his kingdom; he subdues the forces of the kingdom of darkness; he restores those who are sick, and banishes the effects of sinfulness as well as forgiving the sins themselves. This is good news indeed!

Reactions

This message demands a response. If the kingdom of God has come near, and the King himself is already present, life must change. The old lifestyle of indifference to God and his will must be abandoned. Loyalty to the King must be the order of the day. There must be a personal application of the herald's summons: 'Prepare the way for the Lord, make straight paths before him' (v 3). Your life must become consistent with the fact that a King is present.

But how? Jesus gives a straightforward answer: Repent! That is, turn away from your sinful lifestyle, and in the light of my presence live in a way that will please

God. Abandon your old self-centred manner of life, and live the new life of a royal subject.

Was Jesus' message, then, no more than the best possible advice men could hear? By no means! Repentance can never exist on its own. It must always be accompanied by faith. Only through receiving the good news of the King—his proclamation of forgiveness and new power—can we ever turn our backs on sin and live in a way that pleases God. We abandon all our efforts to rule our own lives and establish our own kingdoms, but we succeed in doing that only when Jesus exercises his royal power over us through our trust in him and the message he brings us from God.

Discipleship

The King has come to gather people into his kingdom. Almost casually, Mark tells us of the impact Jesus made on people's lives. In doing so, he illustrates what it means to 'repent and believe the good news'.

Simon and Andrew, James and John were invited to follow Jesus (v 17). Probably the first readers of this Gospel had known Peter well enough, and listened to his sermons frequently enough to know that this was not the first encounter these men had had with Jesus (see John 1:35ff). Mark neither ignored nor deliberately hid that fact. But he wanted to show the challenge to discipleship in its simplest and starkest terms. It means hearing Jesus calling you, and leaving everything for him. For these men that entailed leaving their previous lifestyles and becoming the 'fishers of men' Jesus promised to make them (v 17).

In principle the challenge is exactly the same for us. It may not necessarily involve such a dramatic change in our everyday occupations (although that is by no means infrequent); but Christ's call and his kingly reign over our lives does mean that from then on they are no longer at our own disposal. My family (v 19), my occupation (v 17), even my profitable business partnership—James and John shared a fishing business large enough to employ others (v 20)—all must now be at the disposal of Jesus Christ.

These men were called to be 'fishers of men'. When the picture of 'fishing' is used to describe the activity of God in the Old Testament, it always has an ominous ring to it. God's 'fishing' takes place in the context of judgement. Jesus did not hide that fact from his new disciples. Their mission was to rescue men from the judgement of God. The fact that his reign was already on the horizon leant an air of urgency to the work of those who were to be 'fishers of men'.

Being a disciple of Jesus involves a radical commitment to him and the urgent task of serving him. That is no less true today than it was for Peter and Andrew, James and John.

6

A Startled Congregation

Mark 1:21–28

We traditionally associate Jesus with Nazareth. That was certainly his 'home town'. But there are some indications in the Gospels that, at least for a period of time, he made the city of Capernaum his base. Matthew called it 'his own town' (Mt 9:1).

Capernaum was situated on the north-west shore of Galilee. It was a place of some importance—a tax-office was there; a Roman centurion lived there, indicating that it was probably a military post of some kind. It was there, apparently, that Peter and Andrew and probably James and John also lived (see 1:29).

On the Sabbath (Saturday), Jesus went with his friends to the local synagogue for the service. Jesus was invited to teach during the service. The congregation immediately recognised that there was something completely 'different' about him. Everyone who had been present that morning spoke about his 'authority' (vv 22, 27). It had been no ordinary service. They had seen things and heard things which profoundly impressed them.

WHAT THE CONGREGATION SAW

While he was speaking a man called out to Jesus from the congregation. If you have ever been present at a church service which has been loudly interrupted by someone shouting, you will remember what the atmosphere is like on such occasions. This man was demon-possessed, says Mark, and his attitude was menacing: 'What do you want with us?' he bawled at Jesus.

That kind of language appears in a number of places in the Old Testament. It is that of combat, and it immediately produced a situation of confrontation (see 2 Samuel 16:10; 19:22).

You can imagine what thoughts raced through the people's heads: What would Jesus do? How would he handle this situation? The demon-possessed man continued to shout: 'Have you come to destroy us? I know who you are—the Holy One of God' (v 24). In exposing Jesus' identity, the demon hoped to subdue him in order to maintain his own influence in this poor man's life.

Notice the sense of fear which grips this demon. It seems to sense that the presence of Jesus marks the end of the road. The coming of the King and the inauguration of his kingdom implied the destruction and end of the kingdom of darkness. In its guilt, the demon is terror-struck by what Jesus might do.

We do not know whether or not this kind of outburst had ever happened before in the synagogue at Capernaum. In any case, the situation was an indictment of the spiritual condition of the people. Was that congregation so spiritually dead that it had been possible for a demon-possessed man to attend without being disturbed by what was sung or prayed or taught? Or could it be that this was simply another in a whole series of outbursts against God which the elders lacked the power to withstand?

In the event, Jesus spoke with tremendous vigour and feeling to the demon and commanded him to leave the man. The man shook visibly, and with an ear-piercing shriek the demon left him. Never had the people seen the power of God demonstrated so clearly as this. The tragedy was that they saw Jesus do such mighty works and remained spiritually unchanged. No wonder Jesus later spoke so strongly about the fate of Capernaum (Mt 11: 23–24).

What they heard

We have no details of the message Jesus preached that day. We only know that the combination of his words and deeds had an immediate effect. The people were especially conscious of the 'new' teaching he gave. It was not that he added to Scripture—after all, he had been expounding it. It was the way in which he taught from Scripture, with freshness and directness—the people called it 'authority' (v 26)—which made the lasting impression. It was so different from the usual teaching they heard from the teachers of the law, which seemed second-hand by comparison.

Jewish teaching in the time of Jesus was heavily dependent on what the 'authorities' from the past had to say. Just as a preacher today who quotes constantly from others may eventually give the impression he cannot speak with any authority himself, so it was in Jesus' time. The teaching which depended on the authorities rather than on God's word, ceased to have any sense of authority about it. What God had to proclaim had been hidden by what men had said about it.

Some of these people had been listening to such lack-lustre teaching for years. In all likelihood they did not realise that they were being spiritually starved. No one had been disturbed in that synagogue for a long, long time. But suddenly everything was different when Jesus arrived. They knew now that something had been missing.

It is not too difficult to see the similarities between the spiritual condition of the Capernaum synagogue and that of many of our own congregations. What effect would it have if Jesus were to preach in your church? The tragedy of Capernaum was that they did not listen. Our tragedy is that Jesus continues to speak to us through the New Testament, and far too often we do not listen either.

7
At Home

Mark 1:29–39

Jesus preached about the kingdom of God. In his presence it had come near. He called men and women to turn away from their sinful lifestyle (repent) and to trust and serve him (believe).

The rest of this chapter illustrates, in different ways, Jesus' claim that the reign of God was now being exercised in his ministry.

First of all, Jesus had exercised his royal prerogative to summon men to leave everything in order to enlist in his service. Then he had preached with the authority of God himself, and shown his power over the kingdom of darkness. Now, in this section, he continues to establish his kingdom by deeds of mercy and grace.

A mother-in-law

After the synagogue service that Saturday morning, Jesus went home with James and John to the home of Simon Peter and Andrew. It was then that Jesus learned that Peter's mother-in-law had been taken ill with a fever.

Here, for the first time, we encounter Jesus in one of those run-of-the-mill situations which take place daily around us, and yet for those who are involved in them may be major crises in their lives. Jesus responded by showing his Lordship in this domestic situation. He went to where Peter's wife's mother lay in bed, took her hand firmly, and helped her to her feet. Immediately she regained strength and the fever disappeared. In fact, far from needing a period of convalescence, she ministered to the disciples and even made lunch for them!

This miraculous healing was an act of wonderful compassion on the part of Jesus. But, like all the miracles, it is a clue to the identity of Jesus and the significance of his coming. Think of what happened to Peter's mother-in-law. She was sick and debilitated; her life, however momentarily, had become useless. What Jesus did was to restore her to what she was meant to be, a whole and healthy woman. Thus restored, she served Jesus and his disciples. Jesus restored God's order and purpose to her life. In doing so he gave his disciples a miniature reproduction of the exercise of his kingly rule.

This miracle is a brief glimpse for us of what will happen when the kingdom of God comes in its final form when Christ returns. He will come and restore his world under his authority.

Of course, we do not see this yet. But in Jesus we see that this great reversal has begun (Heb 2:5–9).

After sunset

How much this little group of people must have enjoyed lingering over the meal which Peter's mother-in-law served. What light spirits they must have had, now that their burden had been lifted. But they were not left alone for long. As soon as the sun set, they began to hear voices around the house—crowds of needy people had gathered to seek Jesus' help.

Mark makes a point of mentioning that this did not

take place until after sunset (the Jewish day was measured from sunset to sunset). It was now the day after the Sabbath. The townspeople were, apparently, anxious not to break the Sabbath regulations they had been taught. According to these traditions, helping someone to seek healing might be regarded as 'work' and so it was avoided. In this, Mark gives us a vivid insight into the spiritual plight of the people. Their religious leaders and teachers could not heal and restore them. All they could do was condemn them for 'working' on the Sabbath. By contrast, Jesus taught his disciples the blessings of the Sabbath (and what a blessing they had found this particular Sabbath to be!). He brought healing where the religious leaders could not bring any.

Notice, in passing, that Mark is careful to distinguish in his list of the needy between those who were sick and those who were demon-possessed. It is not true to say that in the Gospels sickness is attributed to demon-possession. Clearly Mark knew that not all sickness is demonic in nature. It requires healing, not exorcism. Jesus distinguished these two things and dealt with them in different ways. He healed those who were sick, and he drove out the demons. He also silenced the demons lest they revealed who he was. (Their purpose, of course, was to create conflict for him before his time to die had really come. So he exercised his royal power and commanded them to be silent.)

Before sunrise

The verses which follow (vv 35–39) bring us into the early hours of the next day, but they are intimately related to the events of the Sabbath in Capernaum. Humanly speaking it must have been an exhausting day for Jesus. But before anyone else in the house had stirred, he had gone to a quiet place in order to pray and spend time in deliberate communion with his Father. He needed to pray that his first day of public ministry in Capernaum would bear fruit, and he wanted to pray over the actions which he was about to take.

How little Peter and the others understood about this. When they eventually found the Lord, they said, with a hint of reproach in their voices, 'Everyone is looking for you!' (v 37). They did not seem to realise that he did not set the course of his life by the whims of the popularity polls in Capernaum. Rather than return to popular acclaim, he shared with his disciples another plan. They must leave the town, for the moment, and go throughout Galilee preaching about the kingdom of God and demonstrating its power. 'This,' said Jesus, 'is why I have come' (v 38). Did he mean 'come from Capernaum' or 'come from God'? Perhaps he meant both. Certainly, both were true. And so, for a time, the little band of disciples went with their Master as he began to announce the kingdom of God wherever they went. He knew why he had come; but it would be some time before his disciples understood it very clearly.

Sometimes when we read passages like this we are too anxious to ask the question: how does this apply to me? What must I do? It is a good thing for us to pause to admire Jesus first. Then we can ask ourselves: do I share his sense of the need for prayer and prolonged communion with the Father? If I know why he came, am I committed without reserve to the service of his kingdom?

8

A Leper Cured

Mark 1:40–45

Leprosy was one of the commonest and most feared of all diseases in the world of the New Testament. The Old Testament law gave detailed regulations about it (eg, Leviticus 13–14). These have led medical experts to conclude that the term 'leprosy' covered a wide variety of skin diseases, including what we today call leprosy. Not only did the leper suffer from the ravages of the disease itself, but he became 'unclean' and was regarded as unfit for society. He was separated from home and family and consigned to a living death, apart from all the blessings of common life. There were few more terrible words to the Jewish ear than to be pronounced 'unclean'. By the same token, to hear the priest pronounce the word 'clean' must have brought relief almost beyond description. That is why the leper in this story asks to be cleansed as well as healed. He wanted to be free from the disease. But perhaps even more, he longed to be free from the stigma, isolation and rejection which belonged to it.

Lepers 'cleansed'

There is something especially appropriate in the fact that when the kingdom of God came in Jesus Christ, lepers were healed and cleansed. Few things more powerfully illustrate what Paul later said about Jesus:

> What the law was powerless to do in that it was weakened by our sinful nature, God did by sending his own Son in the likeness of sinful man, in order that the righteous requirements of the law might be fully met in us, who do not live according to our sinful nature but according to the Spirit (Rom 8:3–4).

The law was powerless to help the leper. If a man were clean, it would not condemn him; if unclean it could not save him. But it was unable to change him. But what the law was powerless to do, Jesus did. Yet, like the entire Gospel which Mark was writing, this story is intended to teach us more about Jesus than about leprosy. There are several things we should notice.

Compassion

First, this story underlines the tender compassion of Jesus (v 41). When this poor man came pleading for help, Jesus was so moved with compassion that he reached out and touched him. Since, according to the rabbis, to touch a leper was to become unclean (even a chance encounter with a leper could render one unclean), voluntarily to touch a leper was almost an incredible thing to do. But Jesus did it deliberately. He wanted to heal the man, of course; but he could have done that without touching him. By touching him, he was really saying: 'I am prepared to become, by choice, what you are by nature—a man under the judgement of the law—in order to share with you what I have—freedom and life.'

As in all miracles, so in this one, Jesus is showing his grace and salvation. He is demonstrating the power of his kingdom. But he is also demonstrating the way in which his kingdom comes: through identifying himself with us in our sin, and bearing the judgement of the law of God against it. He became sin for us, although he was himself sinless, so that we might receive his righteousness in the presence of God (see 2 Corinthians 5:21; Galatians 3:13).

Strong warning

Notice the 'strong warning' which Jesus gave to this man (v 43). He was to keep silent about what had happened. At first sight there may seem to be something almost out of character about this. Why should Jesus speak with such energy and force? The reason he did not want the man to speak was because he knew how easily his miracles would be misunderstood; they would gather a crowd of followers who were interested in him exclusively because he could do signs and wonders. Jesus wanted people to see that his miracles were signs of the kingdom of God, and that it was submitting to the reign of God, not being a spectator of wonders, which really mattered.

Perhaps there is another reason why Jesus spoke so forcefully to this man in particular. Did Jesus see that, despite his faith (v 40), there was something unstable and immature about him? Did Jesus sense that he was just the kind of man who would blurt out every last detail of what had happened? In the event, the stern language proved to be all too appropriate, for the man did exactly what Jesus had urged him not to do. He was the epitome of the person who comes to Jesus for salvation, but then refuses to submit to Jesus because he believes he really knows best how to live his own life (and, alas, often thinks that he knows better than Jesus how to organise the kingdom of God!).

Obedience

Jesus told this man to fulfil the regulations of the law 'as a testimony' to the priests. It may be that the 'testimony' to which Jesus refers was intended to be a witness against these religious leaders. If they recognised the healing, why did they not recognise the Healer? It is also an illustration of the fact that the followers of Jesus do not overthrow the law; they keep the law (see Romans 3:31). But they do not keep the law in the law's strength, for it has power only to condemn, not to change and energise us. They keep the law because the healing and saving touch of Jesus has been on their lives.

How sad it is to record that this man whom Jesus had so wonderfully helped and restored—to whom he had given nothing less than new life instead of the living death he knew before—actually became an obstacle to Jesus. In fact, he became an obstacle to Jesus because of the way he witnessed to him! His life underlines a basic lesson of discipleship: the Lord's work should be done only in the Lord's way, according to the Lord's word. There is no better principle by which to serve him than the one which Mary learned and taught: 'Do whatever he tells you' (Jn 2:5).

9

Only God Can Forgive Sins

Mark 2:1–12

Following the disobedience of the leper whom he had healed, Jesus was forced to remain outside the centres of population. But some days later he returned to Capernaum, which was now his 'home' (v 1). A large crowd gathered at his house there and listened to his preaching. But now, for the first time in the Gospel, Mark introduces a more sinister element. This story, and the four which follow, all have an element of controversy attached to them. They are paralleled by a further five stories of controversy which occur towards the end of the Gospel (11:27—12:37).

The account of the healing of the paralytic introduces us to this hostility to Jesus and crystallises the reason for it.

Bringing the roof down

While Jesus was preaching a group of men brought one of their friends in the hope that Jesus would heal him. Finding the house jammed with people, they had carried him up the outside stairs to the flat roof. They then began to remove a section of the roofing (a less drastic action than it appears to a twentieth-century Westerner!). Determined that Jesus should help their friend, and convinced that he could heal him, they lowered him right down to where Jesus was.

CONTROVERSY

Jesus 'saw' something in these men and their friend—the one thing for which he invariably looked: faith. Immediately he responded, and said to the man, 'Son, your sins are forgiven' (v 5).

That was remarkable for several reasons. In the first place, Jesus obviously spoke to this needy man with exceptional concern and tenderness. By contrast with the teachers of the law who were 'sitting there' (as Mark vividly puts it), Jesus was concerned for people. But, more important, he saw that this man's chief need was to receive forgiveness.

Perhaps his friends were immediately disappointed. They had brought him for visible help, not invisible encouragement! Little did they realise that they were witnessing an event which would eventually lead to Jesus' crucifixion. Nor did they sense that, in fact, Jesus had put his finger on this man's (and everyone's) greatest need: to be cleansed from the guilt of sin.

No doubt Jesus could sense what they were thinking. But he was immediately confronted by the thoughts of another group of men. Written all over their faces were the words: 'This is blasphemy! Who does this carpenter from Nazareth think he is? God alone can forgive sins!'

There was nothing wrong with their theology. They reasoned: since only God can forgive sins, and this man claims to forgive sins, then he must be blaspheming. There was, however, an alternative conclusion: perhaps he did have the authority to forgive sins, in which case he must be...God! But that was impossible!

This was really the heart of the conflict between Jesus and the religious leaders of his time. At one level it became a debate about the application of God's law (for example, the use of the Sabbath, see vv 23ff). But to see it only on that level would be to miss the point. The crux of the controversy was theological, not merely moral. It was about the character of God. The religious leaders were saying: 'God cannot come to us like this and do these things so humbly and graciously. Therefore this man cannot be the Son of God.' The reason they eventually crucified Jesus was because they would not tolerate what his words and works revealed about the character of God—that he saves sinners.

Easier said than done?

They were inwardly accusing Jesus of blasphemy. But Jesus had an answer. He presented them with a challenge: which course of action do you think is easier—(i) saying to this man, 'Your sins are forgiven,' or (ii) saying to him, 'Get up and walk'?

The answer is, of course, that it is easier to *say*, 'Your sins are forgiven.' That is a statement whose truth is difficult to prove or disprove. To say to someone who is paralysed, 'Get up and walk' is to make a statement whose effects can readily be seen. It is the more difficult thing to *say*.

Notice Jesus' logic. He has just said 'the easy thing'. Now to prove that he has the power actually to forgive sins, he says the difficult thing (in the eyes of the religious leaders): 'Get up and walk.' To the amazement of the whole assembly, the man did just that. Jesus had healed him with a word. His action argued for only one conclusion. If his word of healing has been effective, surely his word of forgiveness must have been effective too!

Jesus saw their thoughts; he saw their logic; he demonstrated his divine authority. He was the Son of Man who had the right to forgive sins. 'Isn't Jesus tremendous?' the people said as they went home that day (v 12). The authority of the Son of Man to forgive sins seemed to be exercised so easily. They could not yet have understood that it was an authority given to him because he had come to serve, to sacrifice himself, and to die on the cross to bring men forgiveness.

Here Mark unveils what lies at the heart of the gospel: men need forgiveness; Jesus gives it. The degree to which you see your own need of that forgiveness is the measure of how clearly you understand the gospel.

10

Legalism or Holiness?

Mark 2:13–17

In the story of the restoration of the paralysed man, Mark introduced us to one of the underlying themes in his Gospel: the conflict between the religious leaders and Jesus over the character of God and the offer of forgiveness through Jesus. The four stories which follow continue this theme and, inevitably, share a similar structure: first, the scene is set, then an accusation is laid against Jesus in various ways, and finally, Jesus resolves the issue by an authoritative statement.

LEVI

Following a further teaching session, Jesus walked along the lake shore. He saw Levi (Matthew) sitting at the tax collector's booth. He was collecting taxes for the Roman government, probably on goods which were en route between Syria and Egypt. Tax collectors in general were regarded as 'sharks' and even traitors, since their profession implicated them with the occupying Roman forces. But Jesus called this man to be his disciple. He responded by leaving everything (see Luke 5:28). Mark provides no more details. It seems likely, however, that

Levi had already been exposed to the work and words of Jesus. This call was probably the climax of his pilgrimage rather than its beginning.

It is what follows which particularly interests Mark. Levi invited Jesus and a number of others for dinner. Many of them belonged to the same strata of society as Levi himself. It seems he threw a 'conversion party' to which other tax collectors and 'sinners' were invited. In all likelihood there was a mixture of disciples and 'interested parties'. One would give a good deal to know what the theme of the table conversation was!

The Pharisees

The occasion was not hidden from 'the teachers of the law who were Pharisees' (v 16), and Mark records their reaction. This is the first time the Pharisees appear in Mark's Gospel. They were the spiritual descendants of a group known as the Hasidim (an expression used often in the Psalms for the faithful). They had stood for devotion to the Law, especially when, two centuries before Christ, Greek philosophical and religious ideas had begun to influence contemporary life greatly.

Always a minority group, they held that keeping the Law was a primary religious duty. They also believed that the Law could be adapted to every situation. Their 'scribes' sought to show in what way the Law was binding on each human situation. Eventually they determined that the Law contained 613 commandments (248 positive and 365 negative ones!).

In order to make sure that these commands were fulfilled, the scribes set a 'hedge' around them—adding to them other laws which would protect the faithful from falling into sin. To be a Pharisee, therefore, was to commit oneself to a life of radical separation, and to live in accordance with an enormous list of do's and don'ts.

Among those don'ts was the Pharisees' refusal to buy food from, or to eat food in, the homes of those who were not Pharisees, in case the food they ate had not been tithed, and they should thus break a fundamental principle of the Law.

Jesus was doing exactly what these Pharisees refrained from doing. For all we know this particular group of Pharisees may have asked their question out of real concern for Jesus. They may even have admired many of the things he had said and done. All the more reason for him to break the traditions so flagrantly. Did he not understand them? In any event, it is perhaps significant that they asked (or accused?) Jesus' disciples first, 'Why does [Jesus] eat with tax collectors and "sinners"?' (v 16).

Devastating reply

Our Lord's answer is simple, brilliant and devastating. Had the Pharisees grasped its significance and followed it through, their lives would have been completely revolutionised. Doctors do not visit those who are well, but those who are sick (v 17).

Jesus was teaching these men important lessons.

1. *He was rebuking their misdirected zeal.*

They were concerned for the glory of God and for moral purity, which was commendable. But God's concern for his glory and for purity among men had led him down through history to visit his sin-diseased people to heal them. If the Pharisees were really anxious to see men and women become holy, then their separation to God should have led them to a loving commitment to the people, to show them God's way.

2. He was also exposing their false holiness.

If their so-called 'holiness' expressed itself only in criticism of sinners and not in caring for them, it was not the kind which God wanted, nor the type that Jesus exhibited.

Think of the modern-day surgeon. He 'scrubs up' before his operation. Why is he so careful to be clean? In order to help those who are diseased or physically deformed. True holiness is like that, replied Jesus. My holiness is like that. It is not contaminated by my eating with these sinners. Rather, it seeks to make them whole and holy too.

11

Conflict Continued

Mark 2:18–22

So far in this chapter, Mark has recorded conflicts between the religious leaders and Jesus over (i) the issue of granting forgiveness and (ii) the question of eating with those who disregarded the 'traditions'. Now a third controversy arises, this time over the matter of fasting.

FASTING

The Pharisees fasted—twice a week according to Luke 18:12. They were not slow to point out that the disciples of John also fasted. In view of this, was it not strange that Jesus' disciples did not do so? It is just possible that the question was asked sincerely. But the pattern of opposition to Jesus is too clearly marked in this chapter for that to be likely.

No doubt the questioners were anxious to convey the impression of sincerity. It is not difficult to imagine the scene as they ask Jesus, with all due deference, why it is that his disciples are not fasting. The words contain a thinly veiled criticism of him: how can he be a truly godly leader of this growing band of people when they come third in the spirituality league table, points behind the

Pharisees and even the disciples of John? Clearly John's name could be used approvingly when it suited the situation to do so!

Mark does not stress the exact timing of this incident. In this chapter his order is topical rather than necessarily chronological—these various incidents are probably drawn from different periods in Jesus' ministry.

It is possible that John's disciples were fasting because their leader had been imprisoned. That was no time for eating and drinking! It is equally possible that fasting was a prominent part of the lifestyle which characterised those who gathered round John. He himself was a man of great austerity, and his message was calculated to produce similar austerity in others. While John's disciples did fast, their reasons for doing so were very different from those of the Pharisees.

But the real issue in such matters is always: what does God command us to do? While the Old Testament recorded various seasons of fasting, God had established only one fast day each year—on the Day of Atonement (Lev 16:29–34). Men might fast for many good reasons on other occasions. Jesus himself did—for forty days on one occasion. But to insist on such fasting, as the Pharisees did, was to go beyond the Law of God. And to insist on what God has not insisted on is to seek to outdo God with man-made traditions. If Paul could tell Timothy that Scripture provided all he would need to be a true man of God (2 Tim 3:15–17), adding to that Scripture (as the sects invariably do) is to develop the mentality of the Pharisees and with similar repercussions.

Patches and wine-skins

Jesus would have been perfectly justified in resting his case on the straightforward teaching of the Old Testament. But he took the matter further, and defended his disciples' actions: it would be inappropriate for them to fast. The illustrations which follow explain why.

Jesus' disciples are like a bridegroom's friends. Imagine them fasting when they would normally be feasting in their joy at being with their friend just before his wedding! It would be inappropriate. The time would come for the disciples to fast, when the 'Bridegroom' (Jesus) was 'taken from them'. Mark uses a strong word here, reminiscent of what had been said of the Suffering Servant in Isaiah 53:8: 'By oppression and judgment, he was taken away.' He is pointing, in a veiled way—for those who have ears to hear, to his coming death. Then, when he had been seized, the disciples would indeed mourn.

For Jesus' disciples to fast would be like someone sewing unshrunk cloth on an old garment, or someone pouring new wine into old wine-skins. When the cloth is washed and the patch shrinks, the garment will be in a worse state. As the new wine continues to ferment, it will burst the wine-skins—both wine and wine skins will be lost.

What does Jesus mean? In these final illustrations, he not only emphasises that fasting is inappropriate for his disciples, but that the way of the Pharisees with their legalism and their man-made traditions, and the way of the gospel of grace cannot be harmonised. They are mutually incompatible. Jesus' teaching on God's grace and forgiveness for sinners destroys the old cloth of the Pharisees; it bursts open the old wine bottles of their religion.

The religion of the Pharisees was that God would justify them if they kept the Law and did so by keeping within the 'hedge' their man-made traditions had built around it. It was a religion which depended, ultimately, on the contribution man is able to make to his own salvation.

By contrast, Jesus preached grace, unmerited favour

(indeed, de-merited favour!) and free forgiveness. His gospel began with God; the salvation he preached depended entirely on God. He underlined the difference between this and the teaching of the Pharisees. Now they must choose: God's way or man's way. Which was it to be?

The choice remains the same.

12

Lord of the Sabbath

Mark 2:23—3:6

The series of conflict stories at the beginning of the Gospel draws to a close with two incidents which took place on the Sabbath day.

The weekly Sabbath was simply part of the way of life for the orthodox Jew. It was a day which God had instituted from the beginning of history (Gen 2:2–3). It also stood as a reminder to the people that he was the God of salvation as well as creation (Deut 5:12–15). To abandon the Sabbath day was to turn one's back upon the God of the covenant.

But when the theologians of the Pharisees examined the Sabbath Law, they noticed that it forbade working (Ex 20:8–11; Deut 5:12–15). They therefore asked the question: What exactly is involved in 'working' and how can we make sure that we avoid such 'work'?

Characteristically, their answer involved a lengthy list of regulations which would surround the individual with a 'hedge' to make sure that he was never in danger of breaking the commandment. In actual practice, the breach of these man-made regulations was equated with disobedience to God's Law.

Mark gives us the impression that the Pharisees took

every opportunity to observe Jesus and his disciples in order to 'score' them against their list of do's and don'ts. Here he gives us two illustrations of their scrutiny.

Back to Scripture!

As the disciples walked through the grainfields one Sabbath, they instinctively picked some heads of grain (v 23). This, to the Pharisees, was a form of reaping. Since reaping was working, it was obviously to be avoided on the Sabbath.

Jesus could have answered this accusation in different ways. He could have accused the Pharisees of being ludicrously petty. But they would have then charged him with indifference to the Law. Instead he answered them with a question of his own. Hadn't David entered the house of God and eaten the bread which was to be eaten only by the priests (1 Sam 21:1–6)?

This incident took place when Ahimelech was the priest. It is difficult to know exactly why Jesus says, therefore, 'in the days of Abiathar the high priest' (v 26). Possibly the phrase means 'in the part of Scripture about Abiathar the high priest' (the same phrase is used in this way in Mark 12:26). Alternatively, the phrase may simply mean something like my saying, 'Did you see the film on TV last night in which President Reagan starred?' although it was made many years before he became the President of the United States.

But notice that Jesus is not content to leave the matter here. There is more to this issue than drawing attention to a passage which embarrassed the Pharisees. What lay behind it was a fundamental biblical principle: the Sabbath was made for man, not man for the Sabbath (v 27). It was given to man to meet his needs and to bring him special blessing, not to restrict his life and reduce him to a rule-keeping robot.

The Pharisees were like the committee of a golf-course which had beautiful fairways on which to play. But in order to preserve the fairways from being cut up with divots, they insisted that golfers always play their shots from the rough grass at the side. But golf-courses, like Sabbaths, are meant to be enjoyed, not preserved as living museums. Tragically, the Pharisees were turning the day of blessing into a burden.

A DAY FOR DOING GOOD

The same principle arises even more clearly in Mark 3:1–6. Here is a man in the synagogue with a shrivelled hand. The Pharisees are there, watching our Lord's every move. Will he try to heal this man on the Sabbath?

In full view of his detractors, Jesus commanded the man to stand. Realising what was at stake, he asked a question before healing him: what does it mean to keep the Law of God? Does it mean doing good, or doing evil, saving life, or killing? The point was clear. Jesus was again arguing that God had given man the Sabbath for his blessing. What could be a greater physical blessing to this man than to heal his shrivelled hand? The Pharisees taught that only if the man's life were in danger was healing on the Sabbath permissible—but not otherwise. But observe Jesus' point: why should the Sabbath, of all days, be the one day on which we refrain from bringing blessing to this man? The idea was quite ludicrous!

But there is, perhaps, something yet more profound in what Jesus did. The Law concerning the Sabbath permitted this man great joy, but it could not heal him and restore him to the joyful condition for which he had been created. The scribes and Pharisees could not do that—only Jesus could. As a matter of fact, only Jesus could help this man really to enjoy the blessing of the Sabbath Day. That was something these Pharisees were powerless to do. Perhaps that was why they immediately began to plot how they could destroy him (v 6).

Jesus demonstrated beautifully that he alone is able to give us the grace we need to enter into the joys of obedience to the commandments of God. It is grace which produces true obedience, not legalism.

13

Hostility Abounds

Mark 3:7–12

The antagonism of the Pharisees to Jesus was plain for all to see. No matter how hard they might try to disguise the fact, their questions were deliberate efforts to 'catch him out'. The sequel to their failure to do so is highly significant: they 'began to plot with the Herodians how they might kill Jesus' (2:6). Here were men who were outwardly devoted to honouring and keeping the law of Moses, deliberately planning to commit murder. The reason they needed to 'plot' was in order to do it 'legally'!

The presence of Jesus was showing up some of these Pharisees for what they really were: men who served God with their lips, but whose hearts were far from him (Is 29:13). Before this Gospel comes to an end, we shall hear Jesus himself quoting these words to them.

Twofold error

The great error of the Pharisees was twofold. They had a wrong view of God, and consequently an inadequate view of sin. Unlike the Old Testament prophets and psalmists, they could not see that knowing God meant knowing him in his infinite and heart-searching holiness.

It involved knowing one's own heart in its perversity and self-centredness.

Only when a man sees these two things does he recognise how much he needs the grace of God. Anyone who has ever sensed the real nature of God would not imagine that his favour could be earned by external rules and regulations. On the Lord's authority, Isaiah had declared such 'righteousness' to be 'filthy rags' (Is 64:6). Isaiah himself, perhaps the holiest man of his time, had come to see that he too was a 'man of unclean lips' (Is 6:5) who needed pardon and cleansing.

The Pharisees underlined their inconsistency by joining forces with the Herodians, the supporters of Herod, who for that reason were also supporters of the Roman occupation (see Mark 12:13). How inexpressibly sad that these Pharisees, the 'separated ones', could pride themselves in being 'separated' from rank-and-file sinners, but were prepared to associate with 'upper-class' sinners! No wonder they plotted against Jesus—they could not rest until this thorn in their flesh was removed.

It is against this background that Jesus' withdrawal is to be understood. He knew that the Pharisees were mortally opposed to him. He knew men's hearts well enough to realise they would stop at nothing to be rid of him. But he was not there to march time to the drumbeat of the Pharisees. He was his Father's Son. He followed a heavenly plan and timetable. The time of final confrontation still lay in the future. And so, for the moment, Jesus withdrew (v 7).

Demonic hostility

In the final analysis, there is something demonic about the way the Pharisees attacked Jesus. Their hostility was aroused to such an extent that eventually they lost control of themselves (see Mark 14:65). It is interesting, therefore, that when Jesus withdraws from direct confrontation with them, he finds himself facing a different kind of 'plot' against his ministry.

Crowds flocked round Jesus for healing. Men and women whose lives were dominated by the presence of evil spirits came in large numbers. Mark records their consistent response: 'They fell down before him and cried out, "You are the Son of God"' (v 11).

Why did the demons cry out like this? And why did Jesus silence them? Should he not have welcomed their confession? After all, would people not then be able to say, 'Even the demons recognise his deity?' Why, then, did Jesus clamp down on them with such force? (Mark uses a word here which occurs in the Greek Old Testament in divine rebukes.)

The cry of the demons was a cry of despair, not of faith. It was uttered with malevolence and antagonism, not joy and loyalty. It was calculated to destroy Jesus' influence by suggesting that there was an association between him and those who confessed his identity. What Satan could not do through the Pharisees' rejection of Jesus' claims, he would try to do through the demons' recognition of them. But both men and demons are to be judged by their fruits—and the fruits of both were obvious and profoundly evil.

JESUS' RESTRAINT

By contrast with the confession of the demons, it is noticeable that the Lord showed considerable restraint in revealing his identity. On a number of occasions we find him insisting on it being kept relatively secret. The reason emerges very clearly. The Son of God had come to be the Saviour of men by living and dying as the Suffering Servant. He would only properly be understood and trusted when that dark side of his experience was appreciated. If people thought of him as the Son of God, or even as the Redeemer, without learning *how* he would redeem, they would never really know him. The Pharisees *thought* they knew who he was; so did the demons. But neither understood the real truth of the matter. They saw him only as their Destroyer, not their Saviour.

In fact, there are no other ways to think about Jesus. He is one or the other to you. But which?

14

The Twelve

Mark 3:13–19

Mark's Gospel is characterised by movement and activity. Occasionally, however, he gives the impression of the passage of time by introducing a little section like this one, in which he summarises an important period in Jesus' ministry.

Jesus selected a small group of twelve men to share his life in a special way. He chose twelve as a symbol of the fact that he was building the 'new Israel' out of the old. These men would be the 'brothers' he would use to establish his kingdom throughout the whole earth. As we read Mark's words we should have a sense of thrill in recognising that here Jesus was beginning an 'evangelistic campaign' which would lead ultimately to ourselves and the church in the twentieth century.

Perhaps this is one reason for the extraordinary diversity of the men Jesus chose. There were no 'clones' in this group. By any standard they must have been quite a handful. Who else could have bound together Simon the Zealot (v 18, presumably a strong nationalist before he had become a follower of the Lord) and Matthew (Levi the tax collector)? It was one thing to choose a Simon Peter, but choosing the 'Sons of Thunder' (v 17) along with him was quite a step to take! And then, of course, there was Judas Iscariot who already bears the epitaph 'who betrayed him' (v 19). (He drags it behind him like a chain all through the Gospel.)

Mark tells us that there were three reasons why Jesus chose these men.

Companionship

Jesus wanted men to 'be with him' (v 14). He was a true man himself. It was instinctive in his human nature to desire the companionship of others. He rejoiced in the bonds of their friendship. He loved them, taught them and grieved over their faults. We can even say that Jesus 'needed' them, just because he was truly and fully human—and to be truly and fully human means to be made for friendship. It is never good for man always to be alone (Gen 2:18).

He wanted them to 'be with him' for their sake as well as his own. Only through such intimate contact would they really get to know him and be able to fulfil the task of bearing witness to him. Only in this way would they be fully exposed to the powerful influence of his life and ministry.

In later years, people would be astonished at the apostles' power and wisdom, especially by their knowledge of the Scriptures (despite the fact that they had never studied theology!): 'They took note that these men had *been with Jesus*' (Acts 4:13, my italics). That became the secret of their lives. Through Scripture and by Christ's Spirit, it is still possible to be 'with him'. We should therefore take careful note of the effects of such communion and long for them in our own lives. People thought that the apostles were 'unschooled' (Acts 4:13). They could not have been more mistaken. They had been scholars in the best of schools!

Apostleship

The second reason Jesus chose these men was 'that he might send them out to preach' (v 14). Later in the Gospel narrative they do precisely that (Mk 6:7). But Jesus had a longer term mission in view. These were the men who would continue the ministry he was beginning, of proclaiming the coming of the kingdom of God through his own life, death and resurrection. They would go into the whole world as preachers of this good news.

In some respects, the preaching of the apostles was unique. It was authenticated by 'signs, wonders and various miracles' (Heb 2:4) which were intended to be 'the things that mark an apostle' (2 Cor 12:12). Paul, at least, did not expect that such authentication would mark all preaching down through the ages. These men possessed a unique role in the history of Christ's kingdom which enabled them once and for all to give the word of God (the New Testament) to the church.

But, for all that, there is a pattern in Jesus' dealings with his disciples which he continues to use. He calls us to be with him in order to send us out to others to bring to them the good news of the kingdom of God.

Authority

The third reason Jesus called them was to give them his authority (v 15). Just as he was able to cast out demons, so they would show that the kingdom of God had arrived in the same way. Again this was fulfilled later in the Gospel narrative (see Mark 6:7).

Two things should be noted here. One is that even during Jesus' ministry the gift of exorcising demons was not given to all of his followers. As a matter of fact it was exercised by comparatively few of them. It would be a grave mistake, therefore, to assume that 'exorcising demons' was part of the average Christian's experience in

New Testament times. Furthermore, we should not ignore the real significance of this exorcism. It marked the permanent hostility between the kingdom of Christ and the kingdom of darkness. The whole of Jesus' ministry focused on his destruction of the works of the devil (1 Jn 3:8). He did not come to wrestle merely with flesh and blood, but with the powers of darkness (Eph 6:10–18). The same was true for the apostles. The same is true for us as well.

15

The Greatest Sin of All

Mark 3:20–30

Whenever we read the Gospels we need to pay attention both to what is said and also to the way in which it is said. These books are Gospels, not simply biographies. Consequently, the writers select and present their material in order to convey their message in different ways.

Split screen

Here Mark gives us his equivalent of modern television's 'split screen' (as, for example, in a golf tournament, the two leading competitors may be shown playing on different holes at the same time). He introduces scene one, which centres on the concern in Jesus' family circle over the publicity his ministry was receiving. Their instinct was to take him home quietly, because they were convinced he must have lost his senses.

The second scene pictures the Jerusalem theologians again. They had come down to Capernaum in order to declare the city 'seduced' by Jesus. One of their arguments for this was that Jesus was exorcising demons in the power of the prince of demons, Beelzebub (v 22).

The parallel between these two events is significant

for Mark. They present us with the only possible interpretations of Jesus which are open to us: he is either mad (the family's view) or bad (the Pharisaic theologians' view) or he is what he claims to be, divine (Mark's view).

Theologians rebuffed!

Mark's first focus is on the theologians. He notes the vigour of our Lord's response to them.

First of all, Jesus refuted them. Their criticism is logically incoherent. How could Satan drive out Satan? The idea is unthinkable. No kingdom which is at war with itself can possibly stand. If Satan was really opposing himself, 'his end has come' (v 26). But the one thing which was so obvious from Jesus' confrontation with the powers of darkness was that their end had not come. The devil was alive and kicking.

Strong man bound

Secondly, Jesus provides the true explanation of his ministry. He pictures Satan's victims as the possessions of a strong man. How are they to be taken out of his hands and restored to their rightful owner and former dignity? Only if someone enters the house of the strong man, binds him and then takes possession of the goods. This is exactly what Jesus had come to do—destroy the influence of the strong man, Satan, on people's lives and restore them to their family fellowship with God. Jesus had come into the 'house' of 'the prince of this world' (Jn 12:31; 14:30; 16:11). In his ministry, and supremely on the Cross and through the Resurrection, he would overcome him and liberate his people. That was the true significance of these exorcisms, if only these official theologians had the eyes to see it.

Unforgivable

Thirdly, Jesus followed this teaching with some words of direct practical application. Notice the serious tone of what he says in verses 28–29. There is no sin which places a man beyond forgiveness, no matter what blasphemy may be involved—except one sin: blasphemy against the Holy Spirit.

This statement has sometimes caused readers of the Gospels great distress, and forced them to ask: 'Have I committed the unpardonable sin?' There is nothing trivial about that question. Indeed, Jesus seems to suggest it may be the most important question we ever ask ourselves. But what is blasphemy against the Holy Spirit?

Mark gives a partial explanation. The reason Jesus spoke in these terms was 'because they were saying, "He has an evil spirit" ' (v 30). Here is the one certain sign that a man is in danger of committing this sin—a stubborn resistance to Jesus which eventually expresses itself in treating him as the ultimate evil in our lives.

This sin takes its contemporary forms. It is the sin of regarding conversion to Christ and obedience to him as Lord as the ultimate folly. This was precisely the wilful blindness to Christ and hardness of heart against him which these theologians had begun to display.

It is often said, with some wisdom, that if you are anxious that you have committed blasphemy against the Spirit, you need not fear—for this blasphemy is always accompanied by complete indifference to such sin. But that advice cannot be treated casually, for the person who sins against the Lord, and is at first sensitive to the potential consequences of his sin, may one day be the very person who becomes indifferent to it. The vital thing is to retain that sensitivity throughout the whole of our lives. It can only be retained by keeping close to Christ; and doing so will guard us from such sin.

Mark's Gospel impresses on us that the greatest of sins are often those of the most religious of men. He underlines for us the great lesson that it is not religion, but Jesus, that saves.

16

Christ's True Family

Mark 3:31–35

In the previous section of his Gospel, Mark presented us with a 'split screen'. He introduced one situation and then turned to describe another. In verses 21–22, he allowed us to eavesdrop on the conversation in Jesus' family. But then, as we see them making their way to the crowded house where Jesus was, we find ourselves witnessing a controversy between Jesus and the professional theologians.

But now Jesus' mother and brothers have arrived (v 31). They cannot get into the house because of the crowd. So they relay a message to Jesus. Imagine the scene as the word is passed from one to another through the crowd: 'Tell him that his family is here and they want him to go home—now!'

A SPIRITUAL FAMILY

Jesus' response to the message was totally unexpected. He turned to the crowd, who had presumably heard the message too, and said: 'Who are my mother and brothers, but those who do the will of God?' (v 34). His disciples were his true family!

We do not expect to hear Jesus put family loyalties

into second place. In fact, his words seem a little harsh and unfeeling. After all, his relations were only concerned that he should not make a spectacle of himself.

But Jesus was not being difficult. We know how deeply sensitive he was to his family bonds (see Luke 2:51–52; John 19:26–27). Yet he realised that natural ties are not the only bonds in the world, nor are they necessarily the most lasting ones. They are of great importance (as Exodus 20:12 makes plain), but they do not have priority over our commitment to God's will and his family. Those bonds are the most basic of all. They were in our Lord's life and they must be in ours too.

Jesus turned this crisis in his own life into an opportunity to teach some important lessons about discipleship.

Challenge

He was, first of all, presenting a challenge to his natural family. Yes, they were bound together by blood, by upbringing, by sharing family experiences of joy and sorrow. But Jesus (as Mary and Joseph had known for many years) possessed a higher loyalty to his Father in heaven and to those who belonged to him. No ties of natural affection would ever take precedence over that.

This was an enormous challenge to the disciples because Jesus was saying to them: 'Is your relationship to me "natural" or "spiritual"? Does it depend merely on the "accident" of birth and upbringing, or on your knowledge of who I am and your personal commitment to me?'

The fact that his family feared for his sanity (v 21) does not encourage us to think they had much spiritual insight at this stage of the Gospel record. Jesus wanted them to think seriously about who he really was and what their relationship to him was going to be.

Sacrificial service

Jesus was also giving the crowd an insight into the significance and costliness of his obedience. He called them to put the kingdom of God first in their lives, even before their families (see Luke 9:59; 14:26). But he was not inviting them to a pathway of discipleship he had not walked himself. He himself had left home and family for the sake of the gospel. Those were precious things to him; but nothing would be allowed to stand between him and obedience to his Father. His disciples were to follow him.

Later in the Gospel, Mark gives us a further insight into Jesus' own sacrificial service. Describing his burden in the Garden of Gethsemane, Mark uses the word 'troubled' which in the Greek literally means 'to be away from home' (Mk 14:33). Jesus bore the weight of an eternal homesickness on the cross, for the sake of the gospel.

Encouragements

But Jesus was also giving encouragement to those who were prepared to follow him. Those who do the will of God are his brothers and sisters (v 35). What greater privilege could there be than to be identified with Jesus and his family? We have intimate fellowship with him now, and are even fellow-heirs with him of the glory of God— provided we suffer with him (Rom 8:17).

Jesus was opposed by the religious leaders. He was also misunderstood by those to whom he instinctively looked for support. His family were not the last to try to silence Jesus. The Pharisees, Sadducees, Herodians and Romans all tried to do the same. That was tragic. But even more tragic were those occasions when his own disciples tried to keep him quiet lest the cost of following him proved to be an embarrassment to them. Simon Peter did that on more than one occasion.

Perhaps you are tempted to do the same. If so, remember his words of encouragement: 'Whoever does God's will is my brother and sister and mother.'

17

Sowing in Different Soils

Mark 4:1–20

Most preachers have one particular 'style' of preaching. That was not true of Jesus. Admittedly, he does seem to have taught the same material more than once; he also seems to have had a certain 'style' to his speech. But when we examine his preaching as a whole, we immediately recognise different approaches and styles.

There is, for example, the well-ordered, clearly divided Sermon on the Mount (Mt 5:1–7:29). In a different style altogether is his wonderful discourse in the Upper Room (Jn 13:1–16:33).

But whatever style of preaching Jesus used, one element was constant: he always used parables when he spoke to 'outsiders' (cf v 34).

Parables are mirrors

What are parables and why did Jesus use them? We sometimes say they are 'earthly stories with a heavenly meaning', but that is only partially true. For the parables are more than pleasant stories or Christian versions of Aesop's fables. They reflect the principles of the kingdom of God, and consequently serve as mirrors of our own lives. They force us to ask the question, 'Where do I stand in relation to the kingdom of God?' They show us our own hearts in the light of God's word.

Jesus explained this to the disciples when they asked him about the meaning of the parable of the farmer who sowed in different kinds of soil. In effect the parables were the word of God in seed form, planted in men's lives through Jesus' preaching. Those seeds could lodge in men's hearts and bear fruit. After hearing Jesus speak, a listener might say: 'I knew he was talking about me. I could see myself in that parable he told.' That was exactly what Jesus intended. Just like the parable Nathan told King David (2 Sam 12:1–7), Jesus' parables said to his hearers, 'You are the man.'

Yet people could listen to Jesus' teaching and spiritually be none the wiser. They could 'see' and 'hear' what he said, and yet think of Jesus merely as a story-teller. His stories remained just that—stories and nothing more. They never understood the message they contained. They did not appreciate that they were not listening to a fine story-teller, but to the summing-up of a judge. In fact they were blind and deaf to all God was saying to them (Mk 4:11–12).

Four responses

This parable was the key to all of Jesus' teaching in parables, and so he explained it carefully to the disciples (v 13ff). The seed is the message of the kingdom of God; the soils represent the different conditions of men's hearts (notice that in Palestine, sowing preceded ploughing, as the parable indicates). Those who hear God's word respond in four different ways.

Some people hear the message, but it is like 'water off a duck's back' to them (vv 4, 15). Their minds are full of other things which make them impervious to the gospel. The message of the kingdom simply slides over the surface. Yes, they heard what was said; but the slightest change in conversation will steal away any impression they might have had of God speaking to them. Satan will see to that. He steals away the seed of God's word.

Others seem to respond much more positively. The message fills them with joy (vv 5–6). But as Jesus suggests, this is an inadequate reaction, because a response of joy untinged with sorrow or shame for our sin, or the grief of repentance, is a superficial reaction. Underneath remains the rocky substratum of our hearts which makes them resist the real and lasting impact of God's word. The trials of the Christian life will test the true nature of their response (v 16).

Yet others are like soil which is in many respects good, but is infested with weeds (v 7). No weeding has been done to give an opportunity for growth. Although a crop begins to grow, it is choked.

So it is, Jesus says, with some people who hear the gospel (vv 18–19). They do not allow it to root out sin from their hearts. They hanker after other or better things than they now possess. Eventually their priorities become completely confused. The kingdom of God is crowded out of their lives by the weeds of the world. They did not respond to the so-called 'negative' elements in the gospel (see Rom 8:13; Col 3:5ff). They used no weed-killer, and so the spiritual thorns drain away the supply of life.

By contrast there is the good soil (v 8). Here the seed takes root. Weeding and ploughing is done with a view to the harvest. Sometimes that exceeds all expectation (v 20).

But how do we become good seed? Only by God's grace, as our hearts are ploughed up to receive his word and as we allow its influence to counteract sin in our lives. That means stubbornly resisting the influence of the desire for other 'things', and seeking first the kingdom of God (Mt 6:33).

If there are only four ways to respond to the word of God, to what category does your response belong? That is the question this parable is designed to make us ask.

18

Lights and Seeds

Mark 4:21–34

The parables of Jesus were like missiles launched against the kingdom of darkness in men's hearts. They were 'timed' to destroy the self-confidence of men and women, and to overcome all opposition to their conversion to Christ. They were calculated to bring people to a point of decision. That is why their central theme is the way in which the kingdom of God is established in the world.

We have already seen that the parable of the farmer and the soils was a 'key' one. It was a parable about how parables work. But the word 'parable' in the Bible (*mashal*) has a wide range of meanings. It can refer to a story or illustration (such as the farmer and the soils), or to a word picture, or a wise saying. These different kinds of parable appear in the verses which follow.

The light will shine

'Why do you bring a light into a house?' Jesus asked. 'Do you hide it under a bowl or a bed?' (v 21).

You can almost see the crowd smiling at the very idea. A light is meant to illuminate what is concealed by darkness (v 22). So it is put on a stand so that everyone can see.

Jesus challenged his hearers to think through the significance of this parable: 'If anyone has ears to hear, let him hear' (v 23). He even added another parable: 'Whoever has will be given more; whoever does not have, even what he has will be taken from him' (vv 24–25).

The point of this parable is the contrast between the present concealment of the kingdom of God and its future manifestation. Jesus is among his disciples as a veiled king. But just as a lamp brought into a house is placed where it will shine brightly, so it will be with him. The day will come when Jesus will give light to the whole world (Jn 1:9). He will not remain hidden for ever.

This is why Jesus also stresses the importance of how we hear—now. If we fail to grasp the mystery of the kingdom of God now, and do not respond to it now, we will be increasingly alienated from it in the future. But if we do respond to it, we will grow in our understanding and appreciation and increasingly appreciate its blessings.

The powerful seed

In verses 26 to 29, Jesus tells another of his 'farmer's tale' parables. In the earlier one about the soils, he had emphasised the importance of our response to the message of God's kingdom. This parable shows us that there is another side to the way in which the kingdom is established. It is like the seed which the farmer sows—it possesses its own power to germinate and bear fruit. Whether the farmer sleeps or rises, whether he understands crop growth or not, 'the seed sprouts and grows' and 'all by itself the soil produces corn' (vv 27–28).

Jesus is not contradicting himself. Rather, he is telling two parables, each of which prevents us from misunderstanding the other. Both are necessary to understand the mystery of God's kingdom. The first one emphasised the need for responsive hearts. The second stresses the power of God's kingdom to overcome opposition and establish itself. What Jesus is saying is that from the outside, his preaching and teaching may seem as fruitless an occupation as that of a man throwing seeds about in a field. But it is that activity which eventually produces the crop—because of the power of the seed to germinate in the soil. It may appear to our eyes that nothing is happening. But all the time the seed is at work to produce the harvest.

What an encouragement this must have been for the disciples of Jesus! And what a vital lesson for us too! We do not always see or understand the ways of Christ; but we can have confidence that he is sowing his powerful seed and that it will bear its own fruit. His word 'will not return...empty' (Is 55:11). There will be a harvest.

SHELTERS GROW FROM SEEDS

The closing verses of this section contain Jesus' famous parable of the mustard seed, which was proverbially the smallest seed the people planted (v 31). It was so small that the birds could easily swallow it (and often did, much to the frustration of every mustard farmer and his scarecrows!). Yet that mustard seed could grow into a plant so large that the birds which could have swallowed it would later find shade under its branches.

The kingdom of God is like that mustard seed. Saul of Tarsus and many others since, who were once 'birds of the air', tried to swallow it and destroy its influence in the world. But one day they too came to find shelter in its branches. Think what hope that must have given to the Christians in Rome who first read Mark's Gospel in the face of suffering and persecution. The kingdom would not be destroyed. In fact, one day the Roman Empire which sought to destroy it would seek shelter under its branches.

Think what hope this gives us in whatever part of the world we serve Jesus Christ. We are his mustard seeds today!

19

Ruler of All Nature

Mark 4:35–41

The series of parables Jesus had told described the principles and power of the kingdom of God. In the section which Mark now introduces, he shows us how that power was manifested in real-life situations in the ministry of Jesus.

We have seen that one of the recurring themes of Mark's Gospel is: who is Jesus? Mark constantly draws us into the story of his life so that we ask ourselves that question. Here he tells us how the disciples asked it: 'Who is this? Even the wind and the waves obey him! (v 41).

In the three stories of the stilling of the storm (4:35–41), the restoration of the demon-possessed man (5:1–20), and Jesus' victory over disease and death (5:21–43), Mark invites us to draw one conclusion about Jesus: he is the Messiah; he is God's Son; he is the King. He reigns over the forces of nature and chaos; over the powers of darkness; over sickness, disease, sorrow and even death itself. Jesus is Lord!

But when the disciples took Jesus that evening 'just as he was' (v 36), they had, as yet, little real understanding of him, and no indication of what was about to happen.

They were planning just another crossing of the Sea of Galilee. Some of them were fishermen and knew that lake like the back of their hands. The trip was no more out of the ordinary for them than your daily journey to work. But it was to be interrupted frighteningly by a storm, and ended dramatically with Jesus, the carpenter of Nazareth, demonstrating his Lordship when the fishermen of Galilee were helpless.

The disciples of Jesus were clearly diverted from trusting him by the storm. Their mistake was to focus attention on their circumstances rather than on Jesus. Perhaps it is not surprising that we often make the same mistake when we read this story. We become fascinated by the storm, but the real point of the story is to tell us several very important things about the Lord Jesus.

Jesus leads into storms

The plan to cross to the other side of Galilee by boat originated with Jesus himself (v 35). Crossing over was, for the disciples, simply a matter of fitting in with Jesus' purposes and obeying him.

That underlines one of the most important principles of the Christian life. Sometimes we find ourselves in difficulties because of our own sin and foolishness. But there are times when the Lord himself will lead us into difficulties. Contrary to the picture sometimes painted of the Christian life, Jesus did not solve all the disciples' problems and protect them from trials and perplexities. On the contrary, sometimes he led them quite deliberately into them. This was such an occasion.

It is interesting to think of Simon Peter in this context. Later on he was to write to Christians who were facing persecution: 'Dear friends, do not be surprised at the painful trial you are suffering, *as though something strange were happening to you*' (1 Pet 4:12, my italics).

Was he remembering the trial into which they had been led as immature disciples? Had he begun to learn then that the Lord sometimes leads his followers through dark valleys and difficult places? But why? This passage answers that question too.

THE TEST

Mark describes Jesus in words which must have come directly from Peter, the eye-witness: 'Jesus was in the stern, sleeping on a cushion' (v 38, a fact no other Gospel writer mentions). The squall arose, and the water came over the sides of the boat and threatened to sink it. The disciples panicked, and shouted at him through the wind, 'Teacher, don't you care if we drown?' (v 38) Notice the reply. Having stilled the storm, Jesus asked his disciples, 'Why are you so afraid? Do you still have no faith?' (v 40).

Two issues were at stake in this situation. The disciples had been doubting whether Jesus really cared for them. They had lost faith in his love for them. Hence their question: 'Do you not care?' It was the cruellest question they could have asked, because the very reason he was in the boat, indeed in the world, and the reason he was going to die on the cross for them was precisely because he cared for them. Yet they were not persuaded in their hearts that this was so, and as a result they allowed the storm to come between them and the assurance of their Master's devotion to them. We are like them in many ways. When storms arise, we doubt his love. We allow our faith to be diverted from its anchor in the cross, and lose our moorings in the storms of life. We have so little faith!

The second issue was that the disciples had failed to trust Jesus' word. Jesus had spoken about going over to the other side of the lake (v 35). In the storm, they had forgotten what he said. They had not held on to his word to give themselves the assurance that they would reach the shore safely. They had allowed the voice of the storm to silence the voice of the Lord. Perhaps if they had remembered Isaiah 40:27–31 and 50:10, they would have had stronger faith.

Seeing his glory

Jesus stilled the storm (v 39). His words are reminiscent of the strong language he uses elsewhere in this Gospel to rebuke demons (1:25; 3:12; 9:25). Jesus is subduing the powers of darkness and bringing order out of chaos. But perhaps the most important thing for the disciples was this: for a brief moment they saw the majesty, power and glory of Jesus unveiled. They witnessed his Lordship over nature and its forces. Like men in a storm who see the world momentarily illuminated by lightning and are able to get their bearings again, the disciples saw Jesus 'just as he was', in his glory. It made them realise that if they could answer one question they would have their bearings both for time and eternity: 'Who is this? Even the wind and the waves obey him!' (v 41).

Sometimes we draw from this story the lesson: Jesus stilled the storm in nature, and he can still the storm in our hearts too. That, of course, is true. But it is not the central truth of this passage, for Mark tells us that the stilling of the natural storm raised a spiritual storm in the disciples' hearts: 'They were terrified' (v 41). They had taken Jesus 'just as he was' (v 36), and now they were awed to discover who he really was!

Every test and trial, every storm in life is another opportunity for you to see the glory of Jesus Christ and discover his power in your life.

20

Evil's Bondage

Mark 5:1–13

Jesus had shown himself to the disciples as the Lord of nature by stilling the storm on the Sea of Galilee. Now he stands before them as the Lord of men and the Overcomer of the powers of darkness. But before we look in greater detail at the power and grace of Jesus, we should focus our attention on the man whose name was Legion. He was demon-possessed.

Now, not all men are demon-possessed yet, by nature, all men are ruled by dark and sinister forces (Eph 2:2). In this sense, Legion vividly illustrates the terrible plight of the human condition. It may be that this is the reason the Gospel writers devote a good deal of time to recording the story of his deliverance.

Bondage

The first and most obvious thing about Legion was that he was a slave. His life was dominated by an evil, or (as some translations rightly put it) unclean spirit (v 2). He was the pawn of evil powers, and as a result he was uncontrollable. He did not control himself; and he could not be controlled or subdued by others. People had tried to help him by restraining him with chains (v 4), but all to no avail. With demonic strength he simply snapped them, and carried on his sad life among the tombs. His condition seemed totally incurable. He was destined to belong to a closed world of hopelessness, anguish and despair.

Legion was also utterly alone. He was isolated from the rest of humanity and in a sense alienated from himself as his self-destructive tendencies reveal. He cut himself with stones (v 5). He loathed others; but he also seemed to hate himself (contrast Mark 12:28–31).

Deliverance

When Jesus entered this man's life, two apparently contradictory things took place. On the one hand, he ran to Jesus; on the other, when Jesus began to rebuke the demons, he shrieked at the top of his voice, 'What do you want with me, Jesus, Son of the Most High God?' (v 7). He seemed to know that Christ could deliver him, and so he was drawn to him, and yet he shook with dread at the possible consequences. He simply could not take any more 'torture' (v 7).

Would you not think that a man with such profound need would yield readily to Jesus the deliverer? Theoretically we would. But to think that would suggest we understand the human heart all too superficially. No man yields to Jesus easily by nature. Tragically, like Legion, men often hold on to their bondage in evil rather than yield to the pain of transformation by Christ's power and grace.

This is underlined by the conversation that follows. The man's name, Legion, expresses the fact that he has been used as an outpost of demonic activity in this world. Perhaps, in this military language, we are meant to catch the fact that Satan's opposition to the kingdom of God is not haphazard but ruthlessly well organised. However, not even the gates of hell can prevail against our Lord's onslaught against them.

More value than pigs?

Over the centuries many people have been puzzled by the events that followed, and especially the fact that Jesus sent the demons from the man into the huge herd of pigs grazing on the bank of the sea. Two thousand of them were drowned (v 13). The famous philosopher, Bertrand Russell, pointed to this story in his essay 'Why I am not a Christian'. Why this dreadful destruction? No answer is given by Mark. But there were probably several reasons.

One was to expose the terrible power of these demons and their ultimate goal of destroying whatever they inhabited. By the same token, this holocaust of pigs as the demons took possession of them underlined the enormous power which Jesus had exercised in his authority over them.

But there is another reason. Here was a man who had been held captive in pain and shame by these evil spirits. How could he be persuaded that they would never again be able to enter and dominate his life? How could he be sure that the salvation Jesus had brought to him would never be lost? There was only one way, and Jesus chose it. It is misplaced sentimentality to weep over the destruction of the pigs. It shows that we do not have our priorities aligned to those of Jesus. How strange it is that so many people who enjoy bacon and eggs find this scene so distasteful! Jesus, by contrast, who had taught his disciples that they were of more value than many sparrows, also teaches them that the deliverance of one man is worth two thousand pigs and more!

Legion's story records in capital letters what is true of all men by nature: we are slaves to evil; we are not free;

we are bent, ultimately, on self-destruction. Neither we ourselves, nor others, are capable of breaking the powers which have bound us. Christ alone can break the power of sin in our lives and set us free.

Are you still in the position of saying to him about your own sinful habits: do not send them away (v 10)? Why will you not yield to the pain of Christ's gracious work of deliverance? Why will you hold on to the sin which is destroying you? Your place is with Legion—your mind submitted to Christ, your life given over to your Lord's disposal.

21

Responses to Jesus

Mark 5:14–20

The coming of Jesus to the region of the Gerasenes had brought consternation. No sooner was Jesus on dry land than a demon-possessed man was screaming at him. Within a few minutes, two thousand pigs had gone hurtling to their death, and the herdsmen (whose responsibility they were) had raced back to town to 'explain' to the owners what had happened. In the midst of this confusion, only two people remained calm—Jesus, and Legion. When the townspeople came out, they saw them both—and to their astonishment Legion was sitting beside Jesus, clothed and completely sane. Jesus had made him 'normal' again.

Men made new

In a sense, making people 'normal' again was the essence of Jesus' ministry. He came, he said, to save sinners—to restore men's broken lives by his grace and to repair the ruins into which God's image (man) had fallen. Legion is a perfect illustration of what Jesus does in any life which he enters to possess and transform. He makes men new.

But notice that Mark records two completely different responses to what Jesus did.

Tragic request

Think for a moment about the townspeople. What did they see? There was Legion, a man they all knew. It had been many years since they had seen him look the way he did that day. They had been long accustomed to hearing his shrieks as he ran through the graveyard in the middle of the night (v 5). For years they had warned their children not to play near him. Perhaps they had even used him as a kind of bogy-man to frighten naughty children. There was no greater threat heard by a Gerasene child than 'I'll send you up to old Legion if you don't behave!'

Some of these people were probably related to Legion. Others remembered playing with him in childhood. What kind of response do you think would be appropriate when they saw him gloriously normalised? For years they had not been able to control him, but now he was as biddable as an obedient child. What an occasion for rejoicing!

So we might think. But we would be seriously mistaken. For Legion seems to have been greeted with a stony silence. There was no 'welcome-mat' on the faces of his townsfolk that day. Were they so taken up with gratitude to Jesus that for a moment they forgot Legion? On the contrary. They begged Jesus to leave their shores (v 17).

What possible explanation can there be for such a response to the power of God? A moment's self-examination should give the answer. Jesus' presence had cost the Gerasenes dearly in terms of this world's goods. What had Legion ever been or done to merit the expenditure of two thousand (of their!) pigs for his salvation?

If these were the thoughts passing through the minds

of the people, they were wrong on several counts. In the first place, they did not understand the depths of man's need, or the costliness to Christ of the salvation of men. To 'save' Legion would ultimately cost the Lord Jesus his life. The loss of these pigs was incidental by comparison. But they valued their pigs more than Legion's salvation. In doing so, they revealed that they valued their pigs more than their own salvation, and more than they valued Legion's Saviour.

But there was probably another element in their rejection of Jesus. They could see the radical transformation which Jesus had produced in Legion's life. Did they fear Jesus' continued presence with them because they suspected it would demand a similar transformation in them? Could it be that they would prefer to have Legion demon-possessed and live without Christ themselves? Then it was they who were ensnared and in bondage to the Evil One.

How tragic that men, both then and now, cling to the sins which will ultimately destroy them, and beg Jesus to leave them rather than change them.

YOUR WILL BE DONE

Legion's response was very different. With all his heart he wanted to follow Jesus and be with him. He longed to have Jesus' protecting presence (v 18). Yet our Lord had other plans for him, and refused his request (v 19). He wanted to use him as his permanent apostle to the region of the Decapolis. So he gave him orders to return to his home and family, and to tell them what the Lord had done for him (v 19).

Legion obeyed. It seems that his life left a lasting impression on his people. For later in the Gospel, when Jesus returned to Decapolis, some people brought him a man who was deaf and almost completely dumb (Mk

7:31–37). They believed Jesus could deliver him. Had they learned that from Legion?

Mark presents us here with a contrast which may seem puzzling at first sight. Jesus refused the request of the man who trusted him, but granted the request of those who rejected him. We need to learn that Jesus' refusals to his followers are always because he has some better purpose for us than that which we request. But our refusals of Jesus, when granted, lead to hardness of heart and judgement.

Like the parables, the miracles of Jesus bring us a profound challenge. The challenge of this one is simple: do you want to go with Jesus? Or, do you want Jesus to go? These are the most important questions you could ever answer.

22

Twelve Long Years of Weakness

Mark 5:21–34

Once before we noticed Mark using a 'split-screen' technique in telling the story of Jesus' ministry. He introduces one event, and then, to convey the sense of the passing of time, he describes a second incident. In this section we come to a moving and vivid illustration of this way of story-telling.

It begins with Jairus, the synagogue ruler, pleading with Jesus to heal his daughter. She is already at death's door (vv 22–23). Jesus went with him immediately. There was no time to lose, it seemed. But as the crowd surged forward with them en route to Jairus' house, Jesus suddenly stopped and asked, 'Who touched my clothes?' (v 30).

Everyone touched him

No wonder the disciples were exasperated. This was ridiculous! Of course someone touched his clothes—he was in a crowd. Everyone was brushing against him. What else did he expect?

They should have known better. Jesus stood his ground and looked around the faces in the crowd. To everyone's amazement (and to the horror of Jairus, now panic-stricken that Jesus had stopped), a woman stepped forward, trembling with fear, and 'told him the whole truth' (v 33).

'The whole truth' was that she had suffered from internal bleeding for twelve years, had spent all her savings on 'cures', and was actually getting worse. She was drained of financial resources; worse, she was now drained of all her physical energy. Jesus was her last hope. She had thought, 'If I just touch his clothes, I will be healed' (v 28). So she had come up behind him, anonymously she had thought, and touched him. Immediately the bleeding ceased.

Why, then, did Jesus stop? Why did he raise Jairus' blood pressure and bring such obvious embarrassment to this woman? As we will see, he wanted to teach Jairus a lesson; but he also wanted to give instruction to the lady in the crowd. She needed to know exactly why she had been healed. Jesus was not content that her body should be made whole; he wanted to make her faith clear and strong too.

Weak faith made strong

This woman had believed that Christ's garments could heal her. Jesus taught her that it was he himself, not his garments, that had power to heal. That was why he was conscious that something had happened. Such was his sensitivity that he could distinguish this woman's touch of faith from the pushing and shoving of the crowd. They put their weight into him; she had taken strength and power out of him (v 30).

Our Lord does not explain how he knew this. But he does seem to suggest that he had voluntarily and immediately responded to this woman's grasping for healing. But unless she realised that it was his power, not his clothes, which had healed her, she would remain diseased spiritually, even although healed physically. She would forever see Jesus superstitiously as a healer, rather than intelligently and truly as a Saviour.

Not touch, but faith

The woman had also believed that she could be healed by touching Jesus—and, indeed, when she touched him, she was healed. But Jesus had drawn her out of the crowd lest she hopelessly confuse her physical touching and what lay behind it—her simple trusting. So Jesus explains, 'Your faith has healed you' (v 34). It was not because she had come near enough to touch him, but because she had trusted him that she had been cured.

The church has been very slow to learn the obvious lesson from this story. In the history of the Christian faith people have often substituted nearness to physical objects for saving faith. In the past, so-called relics of the saints, or even of Christ, were paraded before people, or purchased by them, as though they could contribute to their salvation. Recently, people became excited about the Turin Shroud, as though a physical object could be a help to salvation. But Jesus once and for all delivered us from such misunderstandings. It is not his garments which save us; not even touching them saves us (are there not people who might give their right hand for the sacredness of the privilege of touching the Turin Shroud, just in case it might still be the grave cloth of Jesus?). Only faith saves us, because only faith draws on the power of Jesus Christ as Saviour.

Open discipleship

This lady also seemed to believe that she could be healed by Jesus secretly. If only she could touch him in the crowd, no one would know. She is a delightful example of how naïve we can be about discipleship. How on earth could she have kept her recovery secret? Jesus called her out of the crowd to encourage her to take her stand with him. She did not need to be ashamed to confess what had happened. The sooner she did so the greater would be her joy! If she was ashamed to confess Christ now, she might never know the full life which he had given to her.

Mark tells us that Jesus' farewell words were: 'Go *into* peace' (v 34, my italics). That was exactly what she did. She had entered into a new life of wholeness, both physically and spiritually. Now she was to 'go into' it with joy, praising God for all he had done for her. She had 'tried the broken cisterns' and found that 'the water failed'. That day she had discovered that 'none but Christ can satisfy'. It was the greatest discovery of her life. She came for healing and found grace. Instead of slinking away, she was called to rejoice openly in God's grace.

Has Christ ever had any reason to call you out of the crowd?

23

Twelve Brief Years of Life

Mark 5:35–43

Jairus had come to Jesus in the greatest crisis of his life. His daughter was dying. She was only twelve years old, and her life was all that mattered to her father now. That was why he must have been overwhelmed with frustration when Jesus stopped to speak with—a woman! It emerged that she had been healed by Jesus. Why couldn't he just ignore her and get home with him? Furthermore, she had been suffering from haemorrhaging for twelve years—couldn't she have waited another half an hour and allowed his daughter to live? Even now servants were coming from his house to tell him that his daughter had died (v 35).

The fact that Mark records the length of the woman's illness and the age of Jairus' daughter is significant (vv 25, 42). In both cases it amounted to twelve years. Was Jesus trying to teach the synagogue ruler the meaning of compassion? For this poor woman had been drained of energy year after year, just as Jairus' daughter had grown and been healthy. Certainly Jesus was planning to strengthen the faith of Jairus by his teaching to the woman.

A FATHER'S FAITH

Jairus had some kind of faith. Presumably he had heard Jesus speak in the synagogue at Capernaum. We do not know whether he approved altogether of what Jesus had said. He had also heard of, and perhaps seen with his own eyes, some of the miracles. In his desperation, he now threw himself on Jesus' mercy. He appealed to his willingness to come to his aid. He knew that it was not a matter of 'can you?' but 'will you?' (v 23).

TESTING

True faith grows by testing. The good workman tests his work to make sure that it will do all he intends it to do, and take whatever strains it may experience. For that reason, among others, Jesus stopped to speak to the woman he had healed—to test Jairus' faith, as well as hers.

By the time Jesus was speaking to the woman, the messengers had come with the sad news that the little girl had died. Perhaps concerned to see Jairus in the company of Jesus, and anxious in case he should act like a drowning man grabbing at a straw, they encouraged him not to 'bother the teacher any more' (v 35) and to 'come home with us'.

Here was a real test for weak faith. What did Jairus really think of Jesus? Was he, as his servants seemed to indicate, just another teacher? Would he be as helpless as the next man when face to face with life's ultimate reality? Was faith in Jesus good coinage for this life only?

Jesus overheard the servants' words, but ignored them and encouraged Jairus to do the same. He gave two commands: do not fear! Believe! The first was to reassure Jairus that the enemy of death was not stronger than Jesus. The second was to encourage him to hold on to Christ and trust him implicitly. Jairus realised he had no other option. He was 'driven' to trust Jesus in his utter helplessness. That is what true faith means.

STRENGTHENED FAITH

Jesus was urging Jairus to follow the example of Abraham. He too had been faced with an impossible situation: his wife was barren and beyond the age of child-bearing. Abraham himself was as good as dead. Yet God had promised them a son! Paul tells us that Abraham faced the facts of the situation, but he did not allow his actions or thoughts to be determined by his circumstances. Instead he kept his eye fixed on the promise God had given him (Rom 4:18–21). He grew strong in faith as a result.

Jairus was being challenged to do the same. In order to encourage him, Jesus told those who were 'mourning' in the house that the little girl was not dead but merely sleeping. Her condition was only temporary.

That was perfectly true. But faith and unbelief understood it in different ways. The crowd ridiculed Jesus (v 40)—surely one of the saddest statements in the whole Bible. They thought they knew better. Jesus had not even seen the body. But to Jairus it was a word of hope. Jesus believed his daughter would be restored.

In the face of derision, Jairus sided with Jesus. His faith triumphed because he trusted in a triumphant Saviour who showed himself to be Lord of life and death.

THE SECRET

Jesus raised the little girl back to life. He took her by the hand and said, 'Arise!' And she did! No wonder the witnesses were astonished. But why did Jesus act so secretly, taking only the child's parents and his three closest disciples with him (vv 37, 40)? Surely if he had done this in full view of those who mocked him the effect would have been astonishing. He would not only have subdued their pride, he would have created a springboard for evangelism which would have swept thousands into the kingdom of God.

But, of course, that is not true. Those who will not trust Jesus' word will not trust his deeds. The Gospel assumes throughout that intimate knowledge of Jesus is not given to those who despise him. Here one of Jesus' earlier words was being fulfilled: those who do not have (faith) will find that even what they have (the opportunity to have faith, and to see Jesus work graciously in a time of need) will be taken from them (see Mark 4:25).

No doubt the talk in the local inn that evening was about how Jairus' daughter had been 'asleep'. 'Strange,' some of them would say, 'it was just what that Jesus said. Give him his due.' Unbelievers probably never knew what really happened that afternoon. That was why Jesus gave strict orders that her resurrection should be kept a secret among those who believed.

Notice what Jesus did in that little room. He took the little girl's hand (v 41). By doing so—and touching a dead body—Jesus himself became ritually unclean (just as he had done when the woman with the haemorrhage had touched his garment [cf Lev 15]). He shared in her death in order to deliver her from it.

Later, on Calvary, Jesus would share again in death. This time it was our death. He would become 'unclean' for our sake, and bear God's judgement against our sin. In a sense what he was doing here was but a preview of what he would do then. It was also a preview of what he will do at the end of time, when he will take us by the hand and say, 'Arise!' That will not be in secret, but in public: 'Every eye will see him.' Even those who mocked him will see him—and will wail, this time for themselves.

24

Rejection in Nazareth

Mark 6:1–6a

Jesus had been in his adopted town of Capernaum, where at least some of his disciples had their homes (Mk 1:21–34). Now he paid a return visit to Nazareth, the scene of his childhood (Lk 2:51). He was 'accompanied by his disciples' (v 1).

A visit home is always an occasion to look forward to. There is family to visit and there are old friends to see. But Jesus was not visiting for old times' sake. He had brought his disciples with him because he was engaged in kingdom work. That emerged very clearly when, on the Sabbath, he was invited to preach to the local synagogue congregation.

AMAZEMENT

Mark does not tell us what the Scripture reading was that day, nor does he mention the theme of Jesus' sermon. Some students of the Gospels have argued that this incident is identical with the one recorded in Luke 4:14ff. In that case, the Scripture reading was taken from Isaiah 61:1ff. But it seems more likely that Luke records an earlier visit. Here Mark envisages a return visit on which

Jesus found his townspeople no more responsive than they were at the beginning of his ministry.

The amazement of the people was obvious. Wherever Jesus preached people recognised the note of authority and authenticity in his message. He preached biblically, simply, graciously and powerfully. They must have felt what we too feel when we hear God's word properly expounded: 'So that's what this passage means. It's so clear. Why didn't I see it before?'

Resentment

But amazement was only part of their response. Sadly, it was coupled with resentment: 'They took offence at him' (v 3).

There were several elements in this. While Jesus had done miracles elsewhere (in Capernaum, for example, which was some twenty miles north), he did very few miracles in Nazareth. How could he, asks Mark, for people who simply would not trust him? (v 5).

Were the people piqued that Jesus would not put on a demonstration of power for his own folk? They knew that he had worked remarkable miracles elsewhere, but they taunted him about it: 'He even does miracles, how come he's so wise?' (v 2). One can sense the terrible small-town mentality gone badly wrong as they closed ranks in opposition to Jesus.

Much of what they said smacks of pride. Other people might be taken in by Jesus, but they knew better. The implication of their words (vv 2–3) is plain: 'Who does he think he is, speaking with such assurance about God's word and about himself? We'll show him!' Then, in the consciousness that even this would not hurt him as deeply as they wanted to, they twisted the knife in the wound: 'Isn't this *Mary's* son? (v 3, my italics). The innuendo—to a Jew—was plain: even if a man's father were dead, he was still his *father's* son. To refer to Jesus as 'son of Mary' was to cast a stigma on his mother, and on himself. It was to raise doubts about his legitimacy.

Isaiah had prophesied accurately when he said that the Messiah would be 'despised and rejected by men' (Is 53:3). He was, indeed, 'without honour' (v 4).

Jesus had suffered the subtle attacks of the Pharisees with their contorted theological arguments. Here, in Nazareth, the abuse had no subtle nuances. It was open, brazen rejection. They resented and despised him. They could not tolerate one who had come from among them and yet was so different from them. In that respect, Nazareth was a miniature of world history.

Detriment

But their resentment proved to be to their detriment. Jesus had said that the measure we use would be the measure used for us (Mk 4:24). That was tragically true for the Nazarenes. For where people did not trust him, Jesus would not do any miracles. Mark says, 'He *could not* do any miracles there' (my italics)—not in the sense that it was physically impossible, for he did heal some sick folk (v 5), but that it was morally and spiritually impossible. Where the kingdom of God is rejected it is inappropriate for the King to share its new life and joy.

Jesus was 'amazed at their lack of faith' (v 6). This is the only occasion Mark records such a reaction to unbelief. The people of Nazareth enjoyed so many advantages. The Son of God had lived among them in childhood. He had preached to them with power. He had carried out some miracles. It seems likely that he had even returned to them after an earlier rejection (Lk 4:28). But they were blind to his identity, deaf to his message, and hardened their hearts against him. Mark does not record any further visits to Nazareth. Perhaps there were none. Even what they had was taken from them (Mk 4:25).

Let us learn from their sad example.

25

Sent Out by Jesus

Mark 6:6b–13

Jesus had been rejected in his home town of Nazareth. But rejection is never a reason for the servant of God to despair (see 2 Corinthians 4:1–6). Jesus' heart was set on obedience to his Father, wherever that led him and whatever it might cost him. So he did not lose heart. Instead he moved on and began to teach in the various villages (v 1). He saw rejection in Nazareth as the indication of God's providence to spread the good news of the kingdom of God elsewhere.

Fearless or foolish?

Later in the New Testament period, the early church learned from Jesus' example. It kept a proper balance between a fearless perseverance and a foolish persistence. So, here, Jesus tells his disciples to leave the town which does not welcome them.

There is a lesson here for the work and witness of the contemporary church. By and large we have lost the sense of urgency which these early disciples had. As a consequence we often lose their sense of flexibility. We allow ourselves to be engaged in ways and spheres of activity just because we have always done things in this way and in that place. Catching the balance between perseverance and mere tradition is not easy; but it is vital to the advance of the kingdom of God. We always need to be asking if we are using the resources God has given us in the best possible ways. If we retained a sense of the urgency of our task as Christ's witnesses, we would be more likely to be flexible in order to serve him fruitfully.

Clearly this section creates something of a 'pause' in Mark's rapid account of Jesus' life. Its central theme, however, is Jesus' preparation and commissioning of his disciples (Mk 3:14). Two things predominate.

Authority

Jesus sent out his disciples with his own authority (v 7). In Jewish law the one who was sent by another carried the authority of the one who sent him. It was just as if the sender himself had come. Consequently, the treatment received by the 'sent one' (which is what the word 'apostle' means) was understood as the treatment accorded to the sender. These disciples would therefore have been recognised as representatives of Jesus in the fullest possible sense—and those who received or rejected them would have realised they were receiving or rejecting Jesus himself.

This principle was true of the apostles in a special sense. That was why they were able to give the New Testament writings to the church as authoritative Scripture. But there is a secondary sense in which this principle is true for all Christians. We represent Jesus. The reaction of men and women to us as his brothers and servants is their reaction to him (see Matthew 25:40,45). That places on our shoulders a tremendous responsibility to represent him properly. It also gives us a sense of spiritual authority and dignity—it is *King* Jesus we represent.

Manner of life

This responsibility lies behind the further instructions which Jesus gave to the apostles. They were to undertake their mission with the minimum of personal supplies (vv 8–9). They were men with one purpose, and nothing should be allowed to detract from it. Their message was an urgent one: the kingdom of God was near, in Jesus; men should therefore turn away from sin and live in obedience to God (v 12). Everything about their bearing should indicate that their visit would be brief—the villagers must respond now!

For the same reason, when they were welcomed into a village they were to live in the same house until they left. Jesus was not concerned that his disciples would turn up their noses at the food or lack of home comforts they received. That certainly would have brought disgrace on their message. More likely, he was concerned that his disciples should not appear to be on a merely social visit—one night with one family, another with another family, and so on. They were there on the Lord's business, not on holiday. There were times for rest, but this was not one of them.

In a nutshell, the apostles, as Christ's representatives, were to do as Jesus himself would have done. The tone of their conversation, the style of their lives, everything about them was to reflect their master. Everything was to hint at the seriousness and urgency of the message they brought from him.

Even the way they left the village was to express the significance of their visit. If they were rejected, they were to shake the dust of the village from their feet as a prophetic sign. Orthodox Jews visiting Gentile countries did exactly this when they left—shaking off any 'contamination' they might have contracted during their visit. In this action they indicated that the foreign country was outside the sphere of God's holy people and divorced from his grace. In the same way, Jesus was saying that a town which was geographically within the sphere of God's covenant might spiritually be a stranger to it.

What was true then of towns and villages can be true today of denominations, congregations and individuals. The test is: how do we respond to the message Christ has sent to us in his word? How do we react to his authority? How do we treat those he sends us as his servants? Are we willing to repent?

26

A King Enslaved

Mark 6:14–29

We come now to a new section in Mark's Gospel. It extends from chapter 6 verse 14 to chapter 8 verse 30 and records a period of relative withdrawal on the part of Jesus. Mark introduces it with ominous words: Herod had heard of the activity of Jesus and his disciples. No one could predict how Herod would respond. Jesus wisely chose to find some place of relative obscurity beyond Galilee, at least for the time being.

The family name 'Herod' is synonymous in Scripture with opposition to the gospel. It was this Herod's father (Herod the Great) who had perpetrated the massacre of the innocents recorded in Matthew 2:16–18. His grandson, Herod Agrippa, died in the wake of his blasphemy (Acts 12:20ff). The Herod mentioned here bore many of the family traits.

John resurrected?

Why should the name of Jesus strike such fear into Herod's heart? Rumours were already spreading about the identity of Jesus. The powers of the promised new age were already visible in his ministry. Some thought that he might be Elijah, whose return had been promised as the forerunner of the Day of the Lord (Mal 4:5). Others thought he must be one of the prophets returned from the dead. But there was another view: could he be John the Baptist, raised and returned (v 14)? That was Herod's private conviction. But it was not a conclusion based on spiritual understanding. It was the conviction of a guilty conscience, for Herod was the one who had pronounced the death sentence on John's life: 'John, the man I beheaded, has been raised from the dead' (v 16). Now Jesus stood as the God-ordained threat to his indulgence in his sin. Jesus would now become the object of his evil plans. Later in the Gospel, that opposition would come to its bitter fruition (see 12:13; Luke 23:8–12). Jesus knew that the time for his final passion had not yet come, and so he withdrew from Herod's territory.

But why had Herod put John to death? Here Mark explains for the sake of his readers who, presumably, had little knowledge of recent Palestinian history.

John the Baptist had consistently and fearlessly preached his message of repentance. He had applied it with equal consistency to the religious and the irreligious, the great and the lowly—including Herod. Nor had John spoken only in generalities or of trivialities. He had preached that Herod's present marriage to Herodias was contrary to God's law, and thus should be dissolved.

Herod's sin

Herod had married Herodias, his brother's wife. That was clearly contrary to the law of Moses which prohibited marriage to a brother's wife while the brother was still alive (Lev 18:16; 20:21).

Furthermore, Herodias, as her name suggests, belonged to the same family as Herod. She was, in fact, his niece. The law of Moses prohibited the marriage of an aunt and her nephew (Lev 18:13). Certainly some in John's time believed that this was a principle which applied to parallel relationships (aunt and nephew being parallel to uncle and niece). So Herod's marriage could also be regarded as incestuous. There were probably many religious people who were shocked by this. No doubt some of the leaders spoke together privately about it. But John, perhaps alone, had brought the word of God to bear on the situation without compromise. Herod had sinned; he must repent. Repentance could mean only one thing: he must return to living according to God's law and repair all the damge he had done to others as far as that was possible. Notice exactly what John had been saying: 'It is not lawful *for you* to have your brother's wife (v 18, my italics). He had not spoken privately behind Herod's back. He had the courage to speak publicly and plainly to him about his sin.

Herod's conflict

John's preaching had affected Herod and Herodias in different ways. It enraged Herodias. She 'nursed a grudge against [him] and wanted to kill him' (v 19). By contrast, Herod experienced a range of conflicting emotions. He feared John and actually protected him against his wife's plots. He was moved by John's preaching. Indeed he actually 'liked to listen to him' (v 20). Perhaps Herod instinctively knew that John the Baptist was the one man who appeared in his court who told the unadorned truth. Clearly Herod admired John. And no wonder, for John was the first real man he had ever met. So he was torn between his admiration for John, who was all that Herod knew he himself ought to be—but was not, and his bondage to his desire for Herodias.

HEROD'S DOWNFALL

The manner in which the issue was finally settled is very revealing. Like John, Herodias knew Herod's weaknesses better than he did himself. She knew that sin never exists in isolation. Not only was Herod an adulterer; he was full of self-importance and pride. He threw a party which seems to have turned into a ghastly drunken orgy. The men present were prepared to turn the occasion into one of unbridled lust. Herodias was not above using such an occasion for her own ends. She sent in her daughter, Salome, to dance before them. In a moment of foolish public boasting, Herod was so carried away that he promised her anything in return for her performance.

Imagine, for a moment, the noise and revelry, the crude comments of these men, flaming with lust. You can almost hear the silence falling as Salome immediately responded to his foolish offer: 'Give me right now the head of John the Baptist on a platter' (v 25).

Herod was trapped. His men knew it; Salome knew it; Herodias knew it; Herod knew it. There was only one way of escape. He must 'lose face' before all these men and break his drunken promise. But the cost was too high. He would rather lose John than his own pride and desire for influence.

Notice two important lessons this story is meant to teach us.

1. Herod had put off his decision to follow God's word.

He was 'not quite ready for it'. But in the event, the decision was forced on him at a time when he was least ready to make it. In dealing with our sins, there is never a time when we are 'more ready'. We must deal with them now, or we may not be able to deal with them later.

2. Herod seemed to be the prisoner of one particular sin.

In his case it was sexual sin. But no sin exists in isolation. Like so many men, Herod discovered that failure to overcome one diagnosed sin is simply the symptom of failure to deal with sin in general. His spiritual life was eventually ruined by the sin of pride.

No wonder Herod's conscience was so tender when he heard about the ministry of Jesus. But this was more a sense of alarm than a spirit of repentance. The tenderness in his conscience did not last. When he reappears in the Gospels, it is as a hardened man. That was why, when Jesus was brought before him during his trial, he had nothing to say. For rather than seeking forgiveness, Herod wanted to be amused by Jesus: he 'hoped to see him perform some miracle' (Lk 23:8). So he 'plied Jesus with many questions, but Jesus gave him no answer' (Lk 23:9). The real Herod was then displayed: he 'ridiculed and mocked him' (Lk 23:11). Having rejected the preaching of John, he ended life ridiculing the One whom John had said was greater than himself. In the end, God had no more to say to Herod.

The lesson is crystal clear. Unless we silence sin, sin will silence conscience. Unless we heed God's word, the day may come when we despise God's Son—and then God will have nothing more to say to us.

27

The Faithful Shepherd

Mark 6:30–44

The disciples whom Jesus had sent out on mission for the kingdom of God (see 6:6–13) now returned and reported to him. In view of the possibility of opposition from Herod, and the sheer hustle and bustle of life (v 31), Jesus invited them to spend some time quietly together, resting. He was concerned for their well-being as his servants, and in this respect he sets before the church an example to follow.

Thus, the disciple band set sail for a quiet spot. But it was not to be. Such was the impact made by their ministry that the crowds would not let them out of their sight. By the time they had landed, a huge crowd had gathered (v 34).

Compassion

Jesus' reaction to this scene gives us the clue to understanding the miracle which follows. He was filled with compassion for the people because they were like shepherdless sheep (v 34). As the boat pulled into shore, that was probably what these thousands of people literally looked like, their white clothes set against the background of the green grass (v 39). As they rushed towards the landing-place, they seemed for all the world to be like a huge flock of sheep who lacked order, discipline, guidance and leadership. They needed someone to guide them. They were hungry and thirsty for spiritual nourishment; they were straying and lost. How like poor, wandering sheep they were!

Shepherdless sheep

They were supposed to have 'shepherds'. There were priests and teachers of the law, but they had failed to nourish them. Then there was Herod, the king. He should have been the shepherd of the people. Perhaps the setting of this story following the description of Herod is quite deliberate on Mark's part. Herod had thrown a banquet for the rich and famous, and during it had slain John who had been a true shepherd of God's flock. Instead of denying himself for the sake of the people, as their true shepherd, Herod had indulged himself and ignored them.

Jesus stood in marked contrast. Whereas Herod had fed his own lusts, Jesus had compassion on the people and fed them, spiritually and physically. He proved himself to be the Good Shepherd. This is the message of the miracle of the feeding of the five thousand.

Feed the sheep

First, Jesus teaches his disciples that their responsibility is to be shepherds of the people. They are to feed the five thousand (v 37)! We can almost hear their protests echoing through two thousand years of history. Jesus must be joking! It would take the equivalent of many thousands of pounds to buy even the basics to give them a meal (think of the cost of a wedding reception!).

Of course the disciples could not feed them, at least, not in their own strength. But in the strength of Christ they did feed them. What they took out to the people, in a way they never understood, was able to satisfy their hunger. For the disciples, this was but a foretaste of what Jesus planned to do in them and through them in the years to come.

But, secondly, notice how Jesus is the Shepherd of the people. Quite deliberately he gives expression to the thought that had crossed his mind at the first sight of this huge crowd of people: they were uncared for sheep; he would shepherd them. He would reveal himself to them as the Shepherd of Israel (Ezek 34:23).

He arranged the people in groups of hundreds and fifties (v 40)—a reminder of the way in which the flock of God had been organised in the Exodus (Ex 18:21). Then, just as the Lord had given them manna in the wilderness, so Jesus fed these, his sheep.

Perhaps this is why Mark included the incidental piece of information that the people sat on 'green grass' (v 39). It is, of course, another little piece of evidence linking this Gospel to one of the disciples who had been an eye-witness of the event (Peter). But did Mark also see it as an extension of the picture of Jesus as the Good Shepherd of his people, making them 'lie down in green pastures' (Ps 23:2)? It seems very likely. The Shepherd of the Galilean lakeside was the fulfilment of David's most intimate picture of his Lord.

There is another reason why Mark placed this miracle at this point in the Gospel. The previous section, on Herod, had raised the question: who is Jesus? But it had then gone on to describe the murder of John the Baptist. Why did Mark not include the answer to that question then? Because he knew that the next section of his Gospel would answer it. Jesus is the One who has compassion; Jesus is the One who meets men's needs. He is the Good

Shepherd who one day will lay down his life for his sheep. Perhaps some of those whom Jesus fed went home that day, singing with new meaning:

> The Lord's my Shepherd, I'll not want;
> He makes me down to lie
> In pastures green;
> He leadeth me
> The quiet waters by.

28

Jesus Meets All Needs

Mark 6:45–56

The story of the feeding of the five thousand ends with unexplained abruptness in Mark's Gospel: 'Immediately Jesus made his disciples get into the boat and go on ahead of him to Bethsaida' (v 45). Why the immediacy? And why the separation?

Five thousand people represented the population of two of the largest towns in that region. Perhaps Jesus was concerned that if the real secret of the feeding of the multitude became commonly known it would just be a matter of moments before these people would proclaim him to be their long-hoped-for Messiah. He knew that his own disciples had hardly begun to grasp his real ministry as yet; so how much less did the people in general understand? So, rather than be involved in a Galilean uprising, he sent his disciples away quickly, dispersed the crowd, and went alone into the hill country to pray (vv 45–46).

Communion

Mark represents Jesus as 'the Son of God' (1:1). Now he pictures him in fellowship in prayer with his Father. But he gives us no direct insight into the themes of Jesus' prayer-life. We are simply left to draw the conclusion that Jesus needed time alone with God.

How often we comment on this and hear sermons about it, yet how little we do—for ourselves or others—to put it into practice. Jesus was a Man of prayer, and yet he also sought special times of fellowship with his Father, when the strategy of his life and ministry might be reviewed. We need to follow his example. We need to help others to do so as well. Not all mothers, for example, can send their little disciples away in order to have time alone with God! Not all husbands realise that their wives need such times, as they do themselves. At the very lowest level, our Lord's example is an encouragement to build seasons of special communion with God into our lives, and to do what we can to help others do so as well.

But the main point of this passage lies in the difficulties the disciples found themselves in (once again!). 'The wind was against them' (v 48), and try as they might they could not reach the shore. Jesus had noticed this earlier in the evening, but it was not until three o'clock in the morning ('the fourth watch of the night') that he went to their help, walking miraculously over the water.

Mark tells us that Jesus 'was about to pass by them' (v 48). That seems a strange comment until we remember that Mark is probably recording the very words he had heard Peter use in a sermon: 'We saw this strange figure coming to us across the water. We thought it was a ghost. It was about to pass us by, when we cried out.' Jesus reassured them by identifying himself: 'It is I. Don't be afraid' (v 50). He climbed into the boat, the wind died down, and they reached the shore.

LESSONS

This incident was meant to teach the disciples two things.

1. Their own hardness of heart.

'They had not understood about the loaves; their hearts were hardened' (v 52). But what had they not understood about the loaves? They had not learned from the miracle who Jesus really was. Earlier in the day he had shown himself to be the Shepherd of his people. They should have known that he would not abandon them now in their troubles. They should have been trusting but instead they were terrified.

2. The glory of their Master.

Jesus had identified himself with words which must have sounded like an echo in the ears of the disciples: 'It is I', or 'I am he', 'Do not fear'. Where had they heard those words before? Later they would remember that this was the way the Lord characteristically introduced himself to his needy people in the Old Testament. He was 'I Am', the Lord who banished his people's fears.

They should also have remembered what had just happened—when Jesus had organised the people in groups reminiscent of the days of the Exodus, in order to feed them. His actions were a hint to the disciples that just as God had led the people through the Red Sea so that they came to no harm, so Jesus would never let his people perish until their work was completed. Again, he had proved his utter trustworthiness to them. But, like us, they were all too slow to believe it.

Endless needs

The closing verses of this chapter underline one of the themes which Mark has been hinting at all through this section: the quantity and depth of the needs to which Jesus responded. Jesus' arrival in Gennesaret was the signal for an outpouring of need for him from the surrounding towns and villages. Graciously he healed them. Whether in the fourth watch of the night, or the blaze of the noonday sun, he cared for men and women.

Yet, it is apparently possible to see the power and grace of Jesus, and to have hearts which remain hardened. Nearness to him—like that of the disciples—is no guarantee of real trust in him. Even being the recipient of blessing from him is not always the same things as genuine faith in him. Like Herod with John the Baptist, it is possible for us to be hearers of God's word, yet to have hearts which are darkened and hardened towards it.

29

Men Without Grace

Mark 7:1–8

The Gospel of Mark is punctuated by the appearances of the Pharisees. We have already seen them in 2:16, 24 and 3:6 as opponents of Jesus and his teaching. Now they have come down from Jerusalem in order to spy on him. Mark indicates that they came in sufficient numbers to gather round Jesus, perhaps to isolate him from any popular support he might have had (v 1).

No doubt they also wanted to scrutinise his every move, and to do all in their powers to unnerve him. They were accustomed to people being unnerved in their presence. How little they really understood Jesus! He was free from the desire for praise from men which plagued some of these Pharisees. Since he lived in the full light of his Father's presence, he would not be unnerved by their presence.

Caught red-handed!

Imagine the glee, then, in their hearts, when they caught some of the Lord's disciples beginning a meal without going through the ceremony of first washing their hands (v 2). The fact that Mark says 'some' of the disciples were caught red-handed (or better, 'dirty-handed' in this instance!) suggests that these men were quite a mixed bunch.

Mark was writing for a largely Gentile audience, and so he takes time to explain the significance of this (vv 3–4). We too wash our hands before meals, but for hygienic not religious reasons. The Pharisees were less concerned about hygiene and cleanliness than they were about the 'tradition of the elders'. As far as they were concerned, eating with unwashed hands was an indication of indifference to moral holiness. So the Pharisees washed everything—hands, cups and even the kettle!

How complicated the lives of the Pharisees must have been by comparison with the life of Jesus and his disciples. And how child-like the lives of the disciples must have seemed by comparison with the complexity of the Pharisees. That was not accidental. In fact, it takes us to the very heart of the difference between the Pharisees and Jesus. To them, God was a distant Lawmaker who hemmed in the lives of the people. To Jesus, God was the Father of those who trusted in him. He wanted his children to live in open fellowship with him. God's laws express a Father's wisdom.

Read in one way, the Pharisees' words were simply expressions of concern that Jesus' disciples were not following the 'traditions'. But their question (v 5) was a barbed one. Jesus himself was the object of their attack: 'Why don't *your* disciples live according to the traditions of the elders?' (my italics). 'You are responsible for your disciples. They are flouting the "traditions". That means you are flouting the "traditions"' was what these men were really saying.

Notice how Jesus replied: directly, penetratingly and biblically. He quoted Isaiah 29:13 to expose three elements in the Pharisees' lives.

The truth about the Pharisees

1. They were hypocrites

'You hypocrites,' Jesus called them. The word meant, quite literally, a play-actor. In the ancient world, actors did not wear make-up to disguise themselves for the part they played. Instead, they wore masks representing the character. The real personality of the actor was hidden behind the mask he wore. That was the truth about these Pharisees. Their lips said one thing, their hearts spoke a different language altogether. They played a public role of being men devoted to God, when in fact their attitudes and actions demonstrated that they did not really know God at all. We do not need to belong to the sect of the Pharisees to share their sin.

2. Their hearts were distanced from God.

They pretended to be near to God. Their whole lives were regulated by religious duties and activities. But the truth was that they had really set their hearts on someone else: themselves. Their hearts did not beat in time with the love and compassion of God for the needy. That, to Jesus, was the sure sign that they did not really know him.

3. They placed tradition above Scripture.

Isaiah had accused the people in his day of so clinging to man-made traditions that, for all practical purposes, God's word was made subservient to man's word. Jesus saw the fulfilment of that in the Pharisees. To them the observation of man-made external rules had taken the place of inward spiritual graces. Holiness was being judged by what could be seen. But God measures holiness by what is in the heart.

It was not that they had replaced God's love by God's Law. How could they, when love is the fulfilment of the Law? No, they had replaced God's love with self-love, and God's Law with man's tradition. Having made themselves their own gods, they were insisting that others follow them or perish. How thankful Christ's disciples must have been that he had the moral integrity to say as much.

Sadly, the Pharisees had begun as a group of people deeply concerned for personal purity. Their theology was orthodox. But when a desire for holiness, coupled with an orthodox theology is linked to a heart that is closed to God's grace, tragedy results. That is as true today as it was then. Be warned.

30

Hypocrites Exposed

Mark 7:9–16

The Pharisees had renewed their efforts to trap Jesus. Ostensibly they were criticising his disciples; actually they were determined to undermine Jesus' influence on the people. Behind that lay an even more sinister motive. They recognised that Jesus' teaching would destroy their influence and especially their reputation. Jesus was calling into question everything on which they were resting their hopes for acceptance with God, namely the assumption that they were acceptable to him because of who they were and what they had done. It was Jesus' teaching on grace that so enraged them! Jesus taught that God saves sinners. The Pharisees taught, by contrast, that by definition sinners would not be saved.

Grace or merit?

What was at stake, then, in this central conflict in Jesus' ministry was nothing less than the way of salvation. Behind that, of course, lies the very nature of God himself. The Pharisees saw him as one who would be pleased with their keeping of the traditions. Jesus, by contrast, taught that he was a gracious Father, willing to forgive sinners. The Pharisees stumbled at this because it called into question everything they stood for. To follow Jesus, for a Pharisee, would have meant a completely new view of God *and* a completely new attitude to themselves.

There was another reason the Pharisees were so critical of Jesus' teaching. He taught that God graciously saves sinners. But, they argued, if that is so, men will live as they please; they will flout the law of God and yet still be able to enjoy the salvation of God. If only they had been able to see their own hearts clearly they might have seen that the reverse is always the case: it is the man who has been accepted by God's grace who devotes the rest of his life to pleasing him. The man who has no assurance that he is accepted by God will always live a lie, pretending to be better than he is—either before God or men.

At this stage, Jesus did something which few of his contemporaries would have dared to do: he exposed those who opposed him for the hypocrites that they really were. He showed how, for all their proud boasting in their traditions, they were living in disobedience to God's word.

Corban

Sometimes men would take a sacred vow to devote something (money, possessions) to the Lord. The devoted thing then became 'Corban' (v 11), or set apart for God. That was a perfectly good and indeed godly practice.

But the Pharisees gave Corban precedence over God's law. God had commanded his people to love and honour their parents (Ex 20:12). While in normal circumstances a parent will do what he or she can to help the children as they grow up, there are also times when a son or daughter should help their parents. Think, for example, of relatively poor parents whose children 'do well'. As the parents grow old and are perhaps in some need, how fitting it is that children should offer whatever help they can to the father and mother who have poured out their live's energy for their children. It is a beautiful thing to see such care, and a joy to children when they are able to repay in a different coinage the love of their parents.

Jesus envisages a situation like that arising. Here is a young man. He does not anticipate that his parents will ever need his help. So, in his desire to be wholeheartedly devoted to God, he pronounces his possessions 'Corban'. His parents can no longer benefit from them.

But what if some unexpected tragedy strikes, and the parents stand in need? Surely in these circumstances a way must be found to honour father and mother? The ruling of the Pharisees was that nothing could be done, even to alleviate sickness. The tragedy was that the Pharisees actually led those they advised to breach one of the great commandments. Under the guise of religious faithfulness they encouraged disobedience to the Law! On the surface they seemed highly spiritual; but Jesus said: 'You have set aside the commands of God in order to observe your own traditions' (v 9).

Should we not, then, be prepared to put the Lord and his work before father and mother? Indeed we should—and must. Jesus himself taught that (see Luke 14:26). But that never involves indifference to or rejection of the command of God to honour them.

This was just one illustration of the way in which Jesus believed the Pharisees were actually driving people away from God and his word. That was why Jesus spoke with such unusual emphasis. He 'called the crowd to him', he summoned them to listen to him and understand what he was saying (v 14). Holiness is not a matter of externals, but of the heart. It is what comes out of our hearts that makes us unclean, not what goes in.

How very slow the Christian church has been to take Jesus' teaching to heart. But it is too easy for us to point the finger at 'the church'. What about ourselves? Have we substituted the traditions of men for the word of God, and insisted that others do the same?

31

Outside In, or Inside Out?

Mark 7:14–23

The controversy between the Pharisees and Jesus had erupted once again. Jesus had begun to expose their hypocrisy. In ostensibly 'protecting' God's Law with their traditions, they had effectively weakened its radical demands. The effect of their teaching was to give their own regulations priority over the sacred Law of God himself—as Jesus had demonstrated in his discussion of 'Corban'.

Our Lord was concerned about the way in which the people were being led astray by these false shepherds. So he turned from the Pharisees and summoned the crowd to come nearer to listen to what he had to say. He emphasised the importance of his teaching for each of them ('Listen to me, *everyone*', my italics), and urged them to think through its implications ('understand this' v 14). Sin is not the result of our environment, but of the evil in our own hearts. 'Nothing outside a man can make him "unclean" by going into him. Rather, it is what comes out of a man that makes him "unclean"' (v 16).

Superficiality

A major error of the Pharisees was their superficial view of sin. They had almost regulated sin out of existence—or so they thought! But their regulations were simply shutters which blinded them to the heart-searching nature of the Law of God (see Matthew 5:21–48). How foolish they were to think that real holiness and godliness were matters of outward performance! How short-sighted to think that mechanical obedience was what pleased the living God! Yet how common their view of sin was, and is.

The most alarming thing to Jesus was how wide-spread this view of sin had become. The respect (and fear) in which the Pharisees were held was indication enough of that. Even more alarming was the surprise of his disciples at the 'proverb' or 'parable' he spoke. It seemed almost revolutionary to them, never mind to the common people (vv 17–18). They, too, had been overly impressed by skin-deep religion.

Inside, not outside

Jesus patiently explained himself. 'If you will only stop to think about it,' he said, 'you will see that food cannot make you a sinner, nor can abstaining from certain foods make you holy, for it all goes "in one end and out the other"' (v 19)! Food never enters a man's heart.

Clean food

In case his earliest readers failed to grasp the implications, Mark spelled them out. Jesus was declaring all foods 'clean' when he said this. As Christians we are at liberty to eat any food. There may be times when we will abstain from all food, when we fast in order to devote ourselves in a concentrated way to God. There may be foods we will refrain from eating because of their effects on us (the fact that we may eat any food does not mean we are obliged to eat all varieties). We may refrain from eating certain foods on certain occasions because we are conscious of the effect our eating may have on others (see Acts 15:20; Romans 14:14–23; 1 Corinthians 8:1–13). But we remain free to eat all foods as Christians.

The important thing for Mark was the freedom of conscience implied in these words. That freedom is a joy to possess, whether or not we exercise it in any given situation (we do not always need to use our liberty in order to possess it). But that was precisely the kind of freedom which disturbed the Pharisees. Like all legalists who mix 'merit' with 'mercy' in salvation, they would rather carry the burden of these regulations (Lk 11:46) than the light and easy yoke of Jesus' freedom (Mt 11: 28–30).

Unclean hearts

But if Jesus declared all foods 'clean', he also revealed that all hearts are 'unclean'. It is the heart of man (the centre of his being, not the central organ of his anatomy) which is corrupted and pumps sin through every area of his life. It is a factory of evil, including both outward acts and inward thoughts: 'The heart is deceitful above all things and beyond cure. Who can understand it?' (Jer 17:9).

The tragedy of the Pharisees was that they did not know themselves. They had never really asked God to search their hearts to see if there was any offensive way in them (Ps 139:23–24). They did not realise that, at worst, their environment simply 'triggered off' their sinful hearts. It was never the root cause of sin. No amount of protection from 'the world' could ever protect them from the power of sin in their hearts.

Jesus did not mean that outward actions are of no importance—that only the thought counts. For him evil actions are rooted in evil hearts. If we are to deal with the actions we must also deal with the root cause.

GUARD THE HEART

Here Jesus is teaching something many Christians forget. The mere abstinence from certain activities can never make us holy. The battle against sin must be fought within. Since sin finds different outlets in each of us, one individual may need to guard himself in circumstances which do not threaten another individual in quite the same way. But in every heart lie the seeds of every possible sin. Therefore we must root out sin. We must guard our hearts, because out of them come the great issues of life (Prov 4:23).

32

For All Peoples

Mark 7:24–30

In this section of the Gospel of Mark we have already seen that Jesus was under pressure from two different sources: Herod, who feared that he was John the Baptist risen from the dead and returned to haunt him; and the Pharisees, who relentlessly pursued Jesus in their efforts to destroy the influence of his teaching. Eventually these two groups would come together in fulfilment of the words of Psalm 2 (see Acts 4:25–30). In the meantime, Jesus continued to keep on the move in order that his Father's plan for his life should not be thwarted by men.

There is a lesson for us in this. Our Lord knew that his life had been mapped out for him by the Father. It had been foreordained or predestined that he should be crucified. Jesus knew that God's purposes would be fulfilled. Yet, at the same time, he knew he had to live consistently with those purposes. God's sovereign plan did not absolve him of the responsibility to live faithfully and carefully. That is no less true for us too.

Jesus therefore travelled beyond his own country, to the region of Tyre (v 24). Notice that Mark tells us he wanted his presence there to be kept secret. But it was only a matter of time before the 'secret' was out and someone else in need had been drawn to Jesus.

A Gentile woman

Central to the miracle story which follows is that the person who came to Jesus in such need was first, a woman and, secondly, a Gentile. Furthermore, it was not her son who was in need, but her daughter, who was under the influence of an evil spirit. In the ancient Jewish world this was a combination of need beneath the dignity of any true rabbi. In that context we see Jesus restoring this woman and her daughter to the dignity for which God made woman at the beginning—to live as the image of God (Gen 1:26–27).

How much the lady from Syrian Phoenicia understood about Jesus is not at first made clear. She certainly believed he could help her daughter, for she begged him to cast the demon out of her life.

Strange response

Jesus' response has often been a puzzle to students of Scripture. The woman fell at Jesus' feet in her desperation (v 25). Yet Jesus' reply sounds cold and almost harsh: 'Let the children eat all they want...for it is not right to give their bread to the dogs [that is, the household pets]' (v 27).

Two explanations are possible. It may be that Jesus was saying: 'The message I bring is first of all to be given to the Jews, not to you Gentiles.' In which case, the woman's reply suggests that she instinctively saw in Jesus One who was the Saviour of the world and not just the Saviour of his own people the Jews.

The other possible interpretation is this: Jesus had come to this region with his disciples to find rest and haven from the danger of being seen as merely a miracle-worker. The disciple band had gathered to enjoy the fellowship of a family. Should he, the head of the family, interrupt the 'meal' in order to feed the 'household pets'?

If this second interpretation is the right one, Jesus' words are more of a parable than a put down. In speaking this way he was testing out the nature of this woman's trust in him. Did she see him merely as a medicine-man or a magician like so many others? She gave him the answer he was looking for. It revealed a mixture of deep personal respect for Jesus himself, and the firm determination of faith to enter into its privileges: 'Even the dogs under the table are allowed to eat the children's crumbs' (v 28).

What had this woman seen in Jesus' reply which encouraged her to persist in her prayer? Was it his use of the word 'first' (v 27)? He had not closed the door to faith on her part; rather he was gently putting his shoulder to the door to test how firm her faith was. Was it strong enough and real enough to open the door? In fact it was, and Jesus granted her request. She went home to discover her daughter delivered, just as Jesus had said.

The Saviour of the world

Like so many other stories in Mark's Gospel, this one should not be read in isolation. It gives us preliminary hints that Jesus has come for the world, not only for the Jews. But it also occurs in the context of the stubborn resistance of the Pharisees to Jesus. All their education and rigorous efforts to keep the 'traditions of the elders' had blinded them to what this simple foreigner saw in Jesus: she needed him, and she knew he was able to bring salvation to her and her family. The Pharisees would have thought of her not as a household pet, but as a 'Gentile dog', and despised her. The hardness of their attitude to others was really a symptom of the hardness of their hearts to Jesus. They had never been brought to see their need of him. Therein lay the greatest tragedy of their lives. Hardening of the spiritual arteries is a fatal disease.

33

The Deaf Hear, the Dumb Speak

Mark 7:31–37

On more than one occasion already we have noticed that the structure of Mark's Gospel has its own significance. In general terms it is reminiscent of the structure of Peter's preaching of the good news about Jesus. But we have also seen that some incidents are recorded side by side because they present us with the challenge of two different ways of responding to Christ: in faith or in hardness of heart.

In this section of the Gospel, chapter 6:1 to chapter 7:37 seem to follow a pattern which is repeated in chapter 8:1–30. Both these sections begin with a feeding miracle, and end with a miracle of eyes being opened. In this section, it is physical ears and lips which are opened; in the later section it is Peter's spiritual ears and lips that are opened by God to confess Jesus as the Messiah. It is almost as though Mark is preparing us for the great central point in his Gospel when the question 'Who is Jesus?' receives its definitive answer. From that point onwards, the rest of the Gospel will explain the work which Jesus has come to do in his capacity as Messiah.

Jesus and the disciples now made their way back through Sidon to the Sea of Galilee and into the region of the Decapolis (where Legion had so faithfully borne his witness to Jesus). One incident which took place at that time remained firmly embedded in Peter's memory. It appears in no other Gospel. Perhaps it had special significance only for Peter, because he saw in it a parallel to his own spiritual experience.

Without speech or hearing

Whatever the reason for its inclusion in Mark's Gospel, this is one of the most beautiful, as well as being perhaps the most unusual of all the miracles. Picture the scene: a man who is deaf and almost completely dumb is being hurried along by his friends to meet Jesus. Perhaps they are all in such a state of excitement that they have not even explained to their friend what they hope Jesus will do. Excitedly they beg Jesus to heal him.

What does Jesus do? The first thing he does is to take this man away from the crowd. What he was about to do needed to be done privately lest it be misunderstood as some kind of ritualistic mumbo-jumbo. He put his fingers into the man's ears, spat, and touched the man's tongue, looked up to heaven, sighed, and said (in Aramaic, his everyday language), 'Be opened' (v 34).

Sign language

The man could not hear Jesus and he was also incapable of verbal communication. So Jesus 'spoke' to him in the language he could understand—sign-language. The fingers placed in his ears and then removed meant, 'I am going to remove the blockage in your hearing.' The spitting and the touching of the man's tongue meant, 'I am going to remove the blockage in your mouth.' The glance up to heaven meant, 'It is God alone who is able to do this for you.' Jesus wanted the man to understand that it was not magic but God's grace that healed him.

The deaf and dumb man was immediately able to speak and hear (v 35). Why, then, did Jesus urge him and his friends not to speak about what had happened? After all, how could they avoid speaking about it? Clearly the Lord was deeply concerned that his real identity should not be confused. Again he was to be disappointed by the response of those whose lives he had so signally blessed.

All things done well

Yet, hidden in the friends' disobedience is an important lesson for us to learn. For the response of the people to what had happened was that Jesus 'has done everything well' (v 37). There is something quite eloquent in such testimony to him. Perhaps it serves to remind us that even when our witness is not all that it should be, God is able to bring praise to his Son through it.

What, then, did the people find so amazing? The most obvious thing was that Jesus had healed the man. But the manner in which he had done it was also extraordinary. He had done it quietly, modestly and, most of all, graciously. His sign-language was, in a sense, an acted parable of his incarnation—he had entered into this man's world of silence and spoken the only language he could understand.

Deep emotion

But Mark's account includes one element on which we have passed no comment. He tells us that as Jesus looked up to heaven, it was 'with a deep sigh' (v 34). This Gospel is very sparing in its description of Jesus' expressions of emotion. What, then, did this sigh mean? Is it an indication of the energy which Jesus expended in setting the man free? Yet Jesus healed people on other occasions without such sighs. It is more likely that this is an expression of the deep sorrow and anger our Lord felt at the ravages of the Fall in the lives of men. The sigh was the sigh of the heart of God for his needy creation.

Many years before, Isaiah had prophesied that one of the blessings of the gospel era would be that 'the ears of the deaf [would be] unstopped...and the tongue of the dumb [would] shout for joy' (Is 35:5–6). That day those scriptures had been fulfilled in the Decapolis. This man, made to hear the music of God's creation and to speak the praises of the Creator, had been unable to do either. All that was left for him was a stammering attempt to express the deep inadequacies of his humanity for the service of God or man. He shared in the pains of the fallen creation. But now Jesus Christ had made him whole. He was restored, in some measure, to what he was created to be. No wonder the people proclaimed that Jesus 'has done everything well' (v 37).

Prophetic action

Like many other miracles, this one is also a prophecy. It is a glimpse into what Jesus Christ intends to do when he comes again to exercise his reign over all the powers of darkness. By comparison with that day we are all spiritually deaf and only barely stammer the praises of our Creator. It will not always be so. The day is coming when the stammerer will be the eloquent proclaimer of his Father's praise, and the deaf will hear the voice of Christ with crystal clarity.

But that day did not lie only in the future for this man. The joy and power of it came upon him the day he met the Lord Jesus. He began then to hear the voice of God and to speak his praises. So it is for all those who enter with him into the kingdom which Jesus Christ brought so near.

If he had known it, there is no doubt the deaf and dumb man would have sung:

O for a thousand tongues to sing
  My great Redeemer's praise,
The glories of my God and King,
  The triumphs of His grace!

Hear Him, ye deaf; His praise, ye dumb,
  Your loosened tongues employ,
Ye blind, behold your Saviour come;
  And leap, ye lame, for joy!

My gracious Master and my God,
  Assist me to proclaim,
To spread through all the earth abroad
  The honours of Thy Name.

Charles Wesley

34

The Messiah's Kingdom

Mark 8:1–13

We have already noticed that there is a kind of parallel running through the structure of this section of Mark's Gospel. A feeding of a multitude is followed by a sea voyage, conflict with the Pharisees, a discussion which has bread as its theme, leading to a remarkable healing and climaxing in a confession of faith. We will see later that this repeated pattern is of considerable significance for Mark. Through it he is conveying how slow of heart the disciples were to recognise and trust in Christ.

Here in this section, Jesus feeds 'another large crowd' (v 1). There are obvious similarities between 8:1–13 and 6:30–43. In both cases the pattern of the miracle is similar; in both cases the motivation of Jesus is the same—compassion; in both cases there is a plentiful supply of food, miraculously created from a meagre supply of bread and fish.

Two feedings?

It is often said today that somehow the narrative of Jesus' ministry became confused at this point, and this passage betrays a confusion in the memory of the disciples, or perhaps simply a repetition by the author because of a special point he wants to make.

On the face of it, that may seem plausible, but a little thought underlines how unlikely it really is. For one thing, miracles in which thousands of people are fed from a handful of loaves are too memorable for anyone to think it happened twice if it happened only once. The idea is really ludicrous. But further, the discussion which takes place in 8:14–21 assumes there were two feedings. If there was only one, not only is the second story confused, the passage which follows it is a complete fabrication.

Messianic blessings

What is the message of this miracle? It demonstrates the compassion of Jesus, as we have seen. But it is interesting to see this miracle in the context of the ancient promises God had given to his people about the blessings the Messiah would bring when he inaugurated his kingdom. He would supply bread for the hungry. This was how Isaiah had put it: 'You who have no money, come, buy and eat!... Why spend money on what is not bread, and your labour on what does not satisfy? Listen, listen to me, and eat what is good, and your soul will delight in the richest of fare' (Is 55:1–2). When Jesus' coming had been promised, Mary had praised God as one who had 'filled the hungry with good things' (Lk 1:53). Like all the miracles, this miracle points us to the identity of our Lord.

No other resources

There is another emphasis here. In the earlier feeding miracle it seems that the disciples' 'bank balance' was in very good order. 'Are we to go and spend that much [ie eight months of a man's wages] on food?' they asked.

Among twelve of them that sum amounted to two or three weeks' wages. It is not impossible that they had such a sum. It is also possible that this was at a time before Judas Iscariot began to syphon off the funds for himself (Jn 12:6). At the time of the second feeding, however, the disciples had insufficient resources. There was nowhere to buy food in this remote area, even if they had the money. Christ himself was their only resource. For the disciples this lesson was one they needed to learn over and over again.

Signs of the kingdom

This second feeding miracle also seems to have been set in the region of the Decapolis, on the far side of the Sea of Galilee. That distinguishes it from the first miracle, not only geographically but also ethnically and religiously. This crowd was probably a mixed group of Jews and Gentiles, perhaps none of them deeply committed, but awakened by the presence and teaching of Jesus, and hungry to listen to him. In this case, the feeding of the multitude foreshadows the gathering together of those from every nation under heaven to the heavenly feeding of God's people. But it also points to the 'feeding' of the people of God in the church today. Already Jesus was hinting (as perhaps the lady from Syrian Phoenicia had begun to see) that he would break down barriers which separated men and women from fellowship with one another.

No sooner had Jesus left than the Pharisees reappeared, this time questioning him, in the sense of testing him and seeking to trap him. In particular, they wanted some 'sign from heaven' to authenticate his ministry (v 11). For the second time in two chapters, Mark records the deep sighs of Jesus. This time they were of profound anguish at the bitter opposition of these men to himself and his message. Did they want a sign? His whole life and ministry bore witness to his identity. No sign would ever convince such hard-hearted men, therefore none would be given to them. They demanded signs; Jesus showed compassion. If they did not recognise that this was the way God was revealing himself in Jesus, then they must remain in their blindness.

It seems altogether possible that those who were present at the miracle of the feeding did not come to know of its miraculous nature until long after. But the disciples knew, for Jesus used them as his instruments in it. As for the unbelieving Pharisees, they never came to see the power of God in Jesus.

Our own times are no different. But, wonderfully, Jesus is no different either. He is still able to take the inadequate resources we bring to him, bless them, and use us as the instruments of taking his blessings to a needy world. Although our resources be small, and we be few in number, the Lord Jesus is not limited in power. Indeed, he chooses to take the weak things of the world to confound the things that are mighty (1 Cor 1:26–31).

35

No Bread!

Mark 8:14–21

Jesus and his disciples were, once again, on their way back to the other side of the Sea of Galilee, following the feeding of the four thousand. It is not difficult to imagine the scene that follows. Jesus' mind was still full of the experiences of the past hours; perhaps as he enjoyed the natural restfulness of this crossing he allowed his mind to roam, considering the feeding, and the picture this had presented of what would one day take place in his Father's kingdom. This was 'the joy that was set before him' for which he would 'endure the cross' before being set down at his Father's right hand (Heb 12:2).

One loaf

As the boat made its way slowly across the Sea, Jesus sensed frustration among the disciples. Perhaps they were blaming each other for something they had just discovered: they had brought only one loaf of bread with them! At the very least they should have been able to see the humour in the situation. They had just been part of a miracle in which four thousand people had been given enough bread to satisfy their hunger—and they had forgotten to bring bread (of all things!). But, apparently, some of them were really quite upset.

YEAST

Jesus quietly intervened: 'Be careful. Watch out for the yeast of the Pharisees and that of Herod' (v 15). What did he mean? Clearly his mind was still full of the events of his encounter with the Pharisees. Since his disciples' conversation was about bread, Jesus used the 'language' of their discussion to make his point more memorable for them. A tiny amount of yeast affects the whole lump of dough into which it is mixed. The evil and hypocritical hearts of the Pharisees and Herod influenced their whole lives. 'Beware of the yeast of unbelief!' Jesus was saying.

His warning was as necessary as it was timely. The disciples' reaction indicates that their minds were already full of anxiety about themselves and frustration with the providences of their own lives. Just when their hearts should have been lifted up in the joy of being with Christ, they were discontented. How like the Pharisees! They thought that Jesus was blaming them for having so little bread! They, like the Pharisees, were dragging Jesus down in their own minds to their own level!

PATIENT CARE

With infinite patience, Jesus began to pastor his disciples by asking them a series of questions designed to bring them to understand what he was saying. He led them from the content of their conversation ('Why are you talking about having no bread?' v 17), to their spiritual condition—their spiritual blindness and their continued hardness of heart (v 18). Slowly he brought to the front of their minds what he had done in the feeding miracles (vv 19–20). How could they be anxious about having only one loaf, when with them was the One who had fed nine thousand people with twelve loaves, leaving nineteen basketfuls over! They had seen his compassion for those who were in need; could they not trust him to care for them too?

Perhaps into the minds of the disciples came another occasion when they had crossed the Sea with Jesus, and had given violent expression to the distrust and fear in their hearts by asking him: 'Teacher, don't you care if we drown?' (Mk 4:38). In essence that question revealed the same kind of unbelief which characterised the Pharisees and Herod: the refusal to yield to the tender mercy of God in Jesus; the desire to hold on to one's own life and rule it, rather than abandon oneself to the rule and provision of the Lord.

Unbelief

Sometimes we think that only tragedy of major proportions could create hardness of heart and spiritual blindness in our lives. Jesus teaches his disciples otherwise. Here *too little bread* was a sufficient cause to show just how hard their hearts and how blind their spiritual understanding could be. Unbelief is like leaven: small, but influential; apparently insignificant, but all-pervasive in its influence.

Contentment

One of the great marks of true spiritual growth is this: if we know that Christ is with us, we will not wriggle under frustrating providences. Having one loaf was hardly a matter of life or death. Yet its significance grew out of all proportion until it filled the minds of the disciples with frustration, and blinded them to Jesus' presence and teaching. If their hearts and eyes had been fixed on him, they might have been able to smile at their foolishness instead of blame one another for it. The lesson the author of Ecclesiastes taught is one which the disciples needed to learn: 'Better one handful with tranquillity than two handfuls with toil and chasing after the wind' (Eccles 4:6). Knowing and trusting Jesus Christ enables us to live like that, and to say with Paul: 'I know what it is to be in need, and I know what it is to have plenty. I have learned the secret of being content in any and every situation, whether well fed or hungry, whether living in plenty or in want. I can do everything through him who gives me strength' (Phil 4:12–13).

36

The Second Touch

Mark 8:22–30

'Do you have eyes but fail to see?' Jesus had recently asked his disciples (8:18). The stories which follow immediately in Mark's account of the ministry of Jesus describe eyes being opened. There is little doubt that the disciples were meant to learn something about their relationship with Jesus from this miracle story.

A blind man was brought to Jesus in Bethsaida. As on other occasions, people begged Jesus to heal (v 22). Jesus' response again reveals his extraordinary care for and sensitivity to individuals in their need. Later in the Gospel, Mark tells us how Jesus healed a blind man in full public gaze (10:46–52). But here Jesus 'took the man by the hand and led him outside the village' (v 23).

There was a personal and a symbolic reason for this. The Lord's action was a perfect illustration to the disciples of what he wanted to do with them in their spiritual blindness: take them gently by the hand, and lead them on. But there was presumably another reason. Perhaps it was that Jesus understood the personality of this man. Instinctively he knew that to heal him in public would be as painful to him as his present blindness. So he took him outside the village, to a place where they could be quiet together. We would dearly love to know what passed between them during that walk! If you have ever met someone with whom you could share anything, perhaps you have had a taste of the privilege that was given to this unsighted man. Did he pour out the story of his life to Jesus, in answer to his gently probing questions? Did he find himself able to express to Jesus thoughts and fears which he had kept hidden beneath the surface of his mind, even from himself? It seems altogether likely.

Men like trees walking

The unique element in this miracle now took place. Jesus spat on the man's eyes, put his hands on him, and then asked: 'Do you see anything?' (v 23). The question itself is unique. Jesus does not seem to have anticipated complete restoration of the man's sight. When he replied, 'I do see people, but hazily—like trees walking', Jesus placed his hands on the man a second time. Then 'he saw everything clearly' (v 25).

What is the significance of this? Was it that this man was a particularly 'difficult case' for Jesus? That seems unlikely.

Was this miracle then—like others—a sign? Yes! But to whom? To the man? No!—to the disciples. And this is confirmed by the fact that Jesus had already asked them about their vision of him (v 18). He was now leading them by the hand to the point at which their sight would become much clearer, and Peter would confess 'You are the Christ' (v 29). Their spiritual understanding did not come instantaneously, but gradually. They, too, needed the second touch from the hands of their Master.

It would be a great mistake for us to make this miracle, and its message to the disciples, the basis for any doctrine of spiritual experience; for example, the necessity of some kind of 'second experience' in order to enjoy normal Christian experience. Later in the Gospel, Mark records how Bar-Timaeus was given his sight immediately; we do not make his experience the basis for any doctrine of 'one touch experience'. We should avoid the temptation to do the same here. It may be that Jesus' command to this man, 'Don't go into the village' (ie don't go there immediately) was intended to give him time to cope with his experience of healing. We need to do the same, lest we make our individual experiences into norms for all Christians.

Clearer sight

Nevertheless, the lesson for the disciples was this: only as Jesus keeps on opening your eyes to him will you see him clearly. They did have some spiritual vision; but it needed to be healed and sharpened. That would be an ongoing process in their lives as Jesus continued to perfect what he had begun. Indeed, if the 'second touch' symbolised a definite experience for the believer, it would be that of glorification, when we will no longer see only fragments of Christ, but his full glory revealed before us.

In the meantime, our spiritual vision needs to be sharpened. That is why Paul prayed for the Ephesian Christians (who had already received spiritual sight):

> I keep asking that the God of our Lord Jesus Christ, the glorious Father, may give you the Spirit of wisdom and revelation, so that you may know him better. I pray also that the eyes of your heart may be enlightened in order that you may know the hope to which he has called you, the riches of his glorious inheritance in the saints... (Eph 1:17–18).

He recognised that coming to Christ is just the beginning of clear seeing. That is why the prayer so many Christians use before reading a passage of Scripture is not just for beginning believers, but for us all: 'Open my eyes, that I may see wonderful things in your law' (Ps 119:18).

37

Who Is Jesus?

Mark 8:27–30

Mark has now brought us to the turning point in his Gospel. His purpose in writing it has been to enable us to identify Jesus for ourselves.

In the first words of the Gospel Mark had indicated who Jesus was: the Son of God (Mk 1:1). But in the Roman world for which he wrote, being the 'son of God' might mean a variety of things—after all, Caesar himself was regarded as divine! It was essential to explain precisely what he meant. That is why throughout the opening chapters of the Gospel, he has posed the question of Jesus' identity in a variety of ways. When Jesus forgave the sins of the paralytic man who was lowered through the roof, it seemed as if he were claiming a divine identity. Yet the same Jesus who forgave sins ate and drank with tax collectors and 'sinners'! How could any true servant of God do that? (so the Pharisees asked).

Soon the disciples found themselves enquiring about Jesus' true identity, when he stilled the storm on the Sea of Galilee: 'Who is this? Even the wind and the waves obey him' (Mk 4:41). Later in the Gospel, we find that King Herod and many of the people were asking the same question too.

But here we come face to face with the issue of Jesus' identity—on which the entire Gospel depends. For now it is Jesus who asks his disciples questions about his identity.

Notice that there are two stages in the way in which Jesus interogates them.

WHO DO MEN SAY JESUS IS?

First of all, Jesus asked his disciples what others were saying about him (v 27). The answer they gave is illuminating. Some people were saying he was Elijah, others that he was Moses, and yet others apparently listed a variety of Old Testament prophets, including Jeremiah (Mt 16:14).

What was the significance of this? Clearly the people recognised several things about Jesus. He was a prophet. No one could possibly speak as he did unless God had sent him. Like the Old Testament prophets, Jesus spoke with the direct authority of God—people could sense that as they sat and listened to his teaching.

God had promised that one day he would give the people a prophet like Moses (Deut 18:17). Perhaps Jesus was the one? Then, again, God had promised 'I will send you the prophet Elijah before that great and dreadful day of the Lord comes' (Mal 4:5). Could it be that Jesus was the long-promised returning Elijah? Or was he, as King Herod had thought, John the Baptist returned from the dead (Mk 6:16)?

It is interesting to notice with which of the prophets the people tended to associate Jesus. Elijah and John the Baptist were men with the mark of the desert on their lives. We tend to contrast them with the grace of Jesus' ministry. But here we are given a hint that even the people who did not really understand who Jesus was, understood this: Jesus belonged to the same on-going purpose of God as these men. There was the hint of eternal reality in his every word and action.

Was it simple ignorance on the part of the people—or was it perhaps wishful thinking—that they identified Jesus as a preparatory figure? After all, if he were only the forerunner of the Messianic day of judgement which Malachi had foretold, then 'the end' had not yet come. There was still time. Things were not quite that serious, yet. If this were the attitude of the people, they were in grave peril.

Who do you say I am?

It was one thing for the disciples to record the opinions of others. But what about their own convictions? Jesus now faced them with that issue. Who did they think Jesus was? Speaking apparently for the whole disciple band, Peter responded that Jesus was not merely another prophet; he was the *final* prophet, the promised Christ! He was the Son of the living God!

We must not dilute the full force of these words. They come from the lips of an orthodox Jew. Peter and the others had imbibed a fair dose of the teaching of the rabbis. They knew the significance of reciting the great creed of Israel 'The Lord our God, the Lord is one' (Deut 6:4). Peter's confession of Jesus as the Son of God was a breakthrough of monumental proportions. He was saying something revolutionary, not only about Jesus, but about the nature of God! Far from being an 'easy' confession, the kind of thing we might expect from an uneducated first-century Palestinian fisherman, it was the complete opposite. It was the last thing in the world Peter would have been 'programmed' to say by birth or environment.

What had driven Peter and his companions to this conclusion? We can hazard a guess (although Mark does not tell us in so many words). It must have been the same evidence of Jesus' life and ministry which Mark has placed before us already in the Gospel. That point is worth emphasising. You do not need more information than Mark has already given to you by this point in his narrative, to begin to confess Jesus as Christ and as the Lord of your life. He is the one in whom the promises of the Old Testament have reached their fulfilment. His words and works express the authority of God himself. He is the Son of God!

Warning

Jesus closes this section with a warning. His disciples are to tell no one what they have heard and seen (v 30). Why? Should Peter's confession not have been the launching pad for a new evangelistic initiative? Should they not now go throughout the land and eventually to Jerusalem proclaiming openly that the Son of God had come?

Jesus knew that the people would not understand that message. More, he knew that his disciples did not really understand the significance of that message—yet. Certainly, Peter had seen that Jesus was the Christ, the Son of God. He had, at last, seen the answer to the question of Jesus' identity. What he did not yet understand was the nature of Jesus' ministry. In the coming days, Jesus would patiently unfold that to him. But as yet, Peter's poor spiritual vision was only partly healed. Like the blind man of Bethsaida, he needed a second touch from Jesus, in order to see properly. The first touch had enabled him to see Jesus' identity. The second would help Peter to see 'everything clearly' (Mk 8:25). This 'second touch' is described in the rest of Mark's Gospel.

38

Cross-bearers

Mark 8:31–38

We have reached the turning point in the Gospel of Mark. Jesus has given his disciples fresh revelation. Their eyes have been opened. They now know that Jesus is the Christ. That also marked a turning point for Jesus in his sharing of his mission with them. Now that they knew who he was, they must also learn what kind of Messiah he had come to be. The words with which this section begin are, therefore, highly significant: 'He then began to teach them that the Son of Man must suffer...' (v 31). Only when they recognised his identity could they begin to struggle with the way in which their Lord intended to fulfil that identity. He was going to be a suffering Messiah. Mark adds that Jesus 'spoke plainly about this'. It is clear from the response of Peter that the disciples were left in no doubt about the implications of the statement, even if they were slow to believe that things would really happen that way.

SUFFERING SERVANT

How had Jesus come to this conclusion? Mark does not explain. But we know from the Gospel narrative that

Jesus identified himself not only with the promised Messiah; he was also the Suffering Servant, of whom Isaiah had spoken in various parts of his prophecy—the One who would come and be rejected by his own people and die with sinners, but then triumph and be honoured by God (Is 52:13—53:12).

Immediately Simon Peter took hold of Jesus and began to rebuke him for speaking like that! For a moment he had forgotten himself and had begun to speak with the accents of Satan. Jesus rightly rebuked him. His mind was set in a worldly pattern, not in a godly pattern (v 33).

Yet, in another sense, Peter had not 'forgotten himself'. The sad truth was that he was quick-witted enough to see what the implications of Jesus' suffering would be—and he was actually concerned about himself! For Jesus then went on to explain the implications of his identity for those who would follow him. It would mean taking up the cross, losing one's life for the sake of the gospel! No wonder Peter had been so defensive! Jesus seemed to be saying that unless his disciples were willing to commit themselves to this principle of his own life, he would be ashamed of them (v 38).

What was it that Peter had failed to see before which now, for the first time, dawned on him?

The Messiah's ministry

1. Sacrifice

He did not appreciate that Jesus' Messiahship and salvation had sacrifice at its heart. He had never brought together the Old Testament teaching on the Messiah who would bring in the new day of the kingdom of God, and the Suffering Servant who would give justification and forgiveness to God's people. He had thought (in his spiritual blindness) that God's kingdom would come in power, majesty and glory. But Jesus was saying that it would come through rejection, humiliation and shame. What stunned Peter's mind was this thought: God's only Messiah is a Suffering Servant.

2. *Submission*

Peter also failed to see that at the heart of Jesus' ministry lay his complete submission to God's word. Like Satan in the wilderness temptations, Peter was saying to Jesus: 'Yes, you are the Messiah; but choose the way of power to inaugurate your kingdom' (Mt 4:1–11). He did not appreciate that the plan of God is never 'up for negotiation'; it has to be submitted to with a whole heart. Yes, Peter admired Jesus. What he did not yet seem to understand was that Jesus was determined that every moment of his life would be lived in obedience to the Father's plan. Such radical commitment was simply beyond Peter's present experience.

3. *Conformity*

Peter had not yet fully understood that following the Messiah meant conformity to the Messiah. Now it dawned on him: a life of discipleship with Jesus would necessarily involve radical self-denial. The Gospels suggest that this was something Peter found difficult to accept. It seemed just too grim to be true. In fact, so painful was this message to him that on one occasion he responded: 'Look, we have left everything to follow you' (Mt 19:27). Was there not another side to discipleship?

Discipleship is two-sided

In fact, Jesus already indicates here that there are two sides to discipleship. Yes, there is the cross-bearing, the self-denial, the sharing in his sufferings. But Jesus is no man's debtor. Those who lose their lives for his sake will gain them; those who are not ashamed of him or his words will look forward to meeting him again in the assurance that he will not be ashamed of them. Following the crucified Christ means following the conquering Christ who will share with all his people the blessings of his conquest.

Later in his life, Simon Peter seems to have meditated a great deal on Jesus as the 'stone'. To those who believe, this stone was precious. But to others it became a stumbling stone (1 Pet 2:4–10). He knew himself how near he had come to falling on it and being destroyed by it. He learned—the hard way—that there is no other Christ to follow than the crucified one. That is just as true for us as it was for him.

39

Transfigured

Mark 9:1–10

Jesus' summons to wholehearted discipleship had emphasised the cost of following him. Cross-bearing, self-denying loyalty would be the principle of the Christian life. Yet he had already hinted that there was another side to discipleship. Those who lost their lives for his sake would actually gain them. Now, however, Jesus indicates—with tantalising brevity—that the life of discipleship looks forward to sharing in the glory of the Messiah. He said, 'Some who are standing here will not taste death before they see the kingdom of God come with power' (v 1).

All kinds of explanations have been offered for these highly enigmatic words. To what did Jesus refer?

Interpreting Scripture

It is worth pausing to ask a general question at this stage: How should we go about answering a question like that in the course of our study of the Bible? We should first of all look for 'clues' within the passage and its context which will help us to understand the author's words through his mind, not our own twentieth-century mind. Are there any such clues in this passage? The most obvious one lies in the words of verse 2. Six days after Jesus had spoken, he took Peter, James and John to witness his transfiguration. Here Mark clearly draws a connection between what Jesus said and what Jesus experienced on the mount of Transfiguration. He seems to be suggesting that the explanation of this cryptic saying lies in what took place at the end of that week. There three of the disciples ('some who are standing here' v 1) saw the power of God's kingdom, indeed its glory in an altogether new way. It was as though they caught a glimpse of all that Jesus would be when his kingdom finally came. He was transfigured. His glory was seen. His power and kingly majesty were momentarily visible. It was a foretaste of that day when his kingdom would come with power in his Resurrection (when he was 'declared with power to be the Son of God' Rom 1:4). It was a foretaste too of the day of his final glory.

On the mountain

What, then, did these three disciples witness? As Jesus appeared in the radiance of glory, Elijah and Moses came to speak with him. These two great figures of the Old Covenant spoke with Jesus about his forging of the New Covenant in his blood. Luke tells us that they spoke about Jesus' 'exodus', or departure in Jerusalem (Lk 9:31). His death would be the new Passover; the salvation of his people would be the new Exodus. What a fascinating conversation this must have been—paralleled only by Jesus' exposition of the Scriptures on the Emmaus Road on the day of his resurrection! (See Luke 24:13–35)

Peter's excitement

Clearly Peter became so excited he simply had to say something. But how inappropriate his words turned out to be (v 33). He planned to build three shelters. Did this mean that he wanted to erect three 'tents of meeting' here on the mountain on the assumption that the final age had now dawned? Whatever his motive, he had forgotten the words which Jesus had so recently spoken about the cross. Or, had he? Was he perhaps saying in his heart of hearts: 'This is it. The kingdom has come. There is no need for the pathway of suffering and shame. We can stay here with Moses, Elijah and Jesus'?

No wonder God spoke so powerfully, and mercifully in deed and in word. The cloud of the glory-presence of God descended and covered them. The voice from heaven spoke, pointing to Jesus. Did Peter not yet understand who Jesus was, or the significance of Moses and Elijah appearing with him? This glorious moment was not an escape from the cross, but the preparation for it. These two figures should not be thought of as in any sense on a level with Jesus—they were simply witnesses to him. Oh, Peter, focus your attention on Jesus, the Son!

As though to underline this, Moses and Elijah disappeared from view. Only Jesus remained. Peter, James and John had been present at one of the most sacred moments in the whole history of salvation. They had seen 'the kingdom of God come with power' (v 1).

Jesus told them to keep this to themselves until after his Resurrection, and they did. But from time to time these three disciples quietly discussed with one another what they had seen and what their Master had said. They still did not fully understand the presence of God's kingdom in Jesus. Only after the Resurrection would their eyes be fully opened. Then they would understand that the power of God would be made known through the weakness of the Cross, and the glory of Christ made known only through his shame.

The voice still speaks

Would you not give your right arm for the privilege of hearing that voice from heaven bear testimony to Jesus? That is a natural feeling for any Christian. Yet it was not the view Simon Peter eventually took. Later he was to write that the testimony of Scripture to the Lord Jesus is as clear and powerful as any word we might hear from the heavens (2 Pet 1:17–19). By this, he meant that, if we would see the glory of Jesus Christ now we must read Scripture just as eagerly as Peter would have lingered on the mountain top. The same voice speaks in both places! The same testimony is given: Jesus is God's Son; listen to him!

40

What About Elijah?

Mark 9:9–13

As the three disciples, Peter, James and John, made their way down from the mountain where Jesus had been momentarily transformed and they had seen his power and glory, one thing puzzled them. He had told them not to mention what they had seen until after his Resurrection.

Why was this such an enigma? It is natural to assume that it was because they still did not fully understand his mission. Doubtless that is true; but there is more to their puzzlement than this. Like the Pharisees, the disciples believed in a future resurrection (see, for example, John 11:23–4). But for the disciples the resurrection was a sign of the end of the world. It was the forerunner of the final judgement and the new age. If the resurrection was so near, they asked, 'Why do the teachers of the law say that Elijah must come first?' (v 11).

In their minds was the prophecy which had been given through Malachi:

> I will send you the prophet Elijah before that great and terrible day of the Lord comes. He will turn the hearts of the fathers to their children, and the hearts of the children to their fathers; or else I will come and strike the land with a curse (Mal 4:5–6).

As a result, the reappearance of Elijah was expected by many people before the coming of the Messiah, and the end of the ages. Interestingly, some of Jesus' contemporaries thought *he* must be Elijah, because his presence and power did seem to be a sign that God was bringing in his kingdom (see 8:28).

The disciples therefore were puzzled: if the resurrection was to take place soon, what about the promised coming of Elijah? Were the teachers wrong?

Who is Elijah?

'No', answered Jesus. They were not wrong in their expectation; but they were shortsighted in their interpretation of the prophecy. Elijah does come first and his work is restoration (v 12). But, says Jesus (notice how gently he leads them to a true understanding of the Scriptures!), that Old Testament passage cannot be isolated from other passages about God's kingdom. Scripture also says that the 'Son of Man must suffer much and be rejected' (v 12). How can these things be harmonised?

John the Baptist was Elijah. The restoration in which he engaged was not a physical restoration, because the kingdom he served was not a political one. He preached a restoration of repentance, of changed hearts, not of worldly power and might. The response to him was but a foreshadowing of the response there would be to the Messiah—rejection.

To the 'inner circle' of the disciples who heard this, Jesus' words must have been breathtaking in their significance. For once, all the scriptures made sense. The political and worldly interpretations which had been placed on the hope of the Messiah's kingdom were overturned. Elijah had already come! But the people had been blind to him, just as they would be also to the One whose kingdom the new Elijah had proclaimed.

The resurrection of which Jesus had spoken was not that of the end of the world, but rather that of the beginning of the new world, and the new race of men and women who would be followers of Jesus. Then, but not before then, would it be fitting to share with others what had been revealed on the mountain top. The resurrection of which he spoke was his own victory over the powers of darkness and death.

Slow to understand

This section underlines a theme we have already noticed running through Mark's Gospel. Jesus' disciples trusted and loved him. They really did believe that he was the Christ. But how little they understood what that really meant. They had been guilty of interpreting the Scriptures in terms of the traditions they had heard and their own ideas. Now, almost daily, it seemed as though Jesus was showing them things in the Scriptures they had been blinded to before. That was a ministry he would continue even after the Resurrection (Lk 24:25–27, 34).

There is a lesson for us here. We are also prone to interpret God's word badly. Our great need is for Jesus himself to explain to us what it means. He is the One who can touch our eyes again and again, to help us to see (cf Mk 8:22–6). He uses all kinds of instruments to do so: sermons, books, study groups, private reading, friends and so on. But in the last analysis it is only Jesus himself who can open our eyes to see what the Lord is saying to us in his word. That is why the promise he has given to the church of the presence of the Holy Spirit—Jesus' own Spirit—as our teacher, is so priceless. It is his presence that makes our hearts burn within us as the Scriptures are expounded (Lk 24:34)!

41

Man's Failure, Christ's Faith

Mark 9:14–29

The artist Raphael's unfinished last work was a painting of the dual scene of the Mount of Transfiguration and the valley below it. On the mountain top, the light of glory shines as Christ appears in his majesty; in the valley there is only gloom and darkness because the disciples have no power to help a dire case of human need (v 18).

Disciples' failure

An argument had broken out between the disciples and the teachers of the law. The focus of the argument involved helping this young boy who was deaf and dumb, and also suffered from seizures of a severe and destructive nature. His father had come to Jesus' disciples asking them to drive out the evil spirit in his son, and to set him free for life. But they could not do it. Perhaps it was their failure which had led to their argument with the teachers of the law. But just then, Jesus arrived.

Mark vividly captures the pressures and frustrations of Christ's life in these verses. On the mountain top he had been faced with the spiritual short-sightedness of his disciples. Here in the valley he was confronted by unbelief, and asked, 'O unbelieving generation, how long shall I stay with you? How long shall I put up with you? (v 19). That cry from the heart is very significant. It underlines for us the very real disappointment which Jesus felt with his disciples. He did not 'soft-pedal' his reactions. Nor did he allow them to think of their failure as a justifiable inadequacy ('We're only human, after all'). No; it was *unbelief*.

The boy's condition

Clearly Jesus did not regard this boy's condition as 'ordinary' epilepsy (not that any epilepsy can be 'ordinary' for those who suffer from it). He shared with the father the conviction that the cause of these seizures, and of the boy's hearing and speech defects, was demonic. This was confirmed when the lad was brought to Jesus and was immediately convulsed by the evil spirit.

The Lord asked how long he had been in this condition. The answer, 'from childhood' and the description of how the spirit often seemed to throw him into the fire or into water must have moved Jesus deeply. He was an only son (Lk 9:38); he had been afflicted in this way since his childhood; the seizures came 'often' (v 21). As a deaf mute, he could not hear the words of comfort his father must often have mouthed to him and could not speak to share the inner despair he must so frequently have felt.

Jesus is Lord

Notice that Jesus did two important things: first he rebuked the evil spirit (v 25). As King and judge of all things, Jesus issued his judgement of guilt and condemnation on this spirit; then he commanded the spirit to leave and never to return. He declared the boy to be permanently free from such demonic influence for the rest of his life. In doing so he not only dealt with the root of his need but also brought him into a fearless enjoyment of freedom!

So violent was the departure of the spirit that the crowd thought for a moment that the boy was dead (v 26). But when Jesus took him by the hand, 'he stood up'. The word here is the word for 'resurrection'. The boy had truly been given new life. But, as we shall see, the use of 'resurrection language' is a signpost from Mark about the ultimate significance of this miracle.

Conversations

Running alongside the action in this story are two important conversations: one between Jesus and the boy's father, the other between Jesus and the disciples.

1. *The need for faith*

Disappointed by the disciples' failures, the father had asked Jesus to help 'if you can'. Jesus challenges the weakness of his faith: 'Everything is possible for the one who believes' (v 23). But what does he mean? Does he mean that the boy will be delivered if the father has faith? Or, does he mean that the boy can be delivered because Jesus has faith and is therefore able to set him free? Either interpretation is possible. In any event, the father's weak faith was strengthened. 'I too believe' he said, 'because you have such perfect trust in the power of God, help me to cast out my unbelief and trust fully in him' (v 24).

But why did Jesus place such emphasis on faith? Because he wanted the blessing this family was about to receive to be experienced in the context of personal trust in him and love for him. That is always his way, whether he brings deliverance to us or not.

2. The nature of faith

Why had the disciples been unable to drive out the demon (vv 18, 28)? Only prayer could do this, replied Jesus (v 29). The disciples had relied on their own strength, or perhaps on their past achievements (eg Mark 6:13) instead of calling on the power of God. But that is what faith in action is. Faith is man in his weakness trusting God's promise in his word. Only through such weakness is the strength of God seen.

Jesus delivered this boy by 'weakness', that is by relying in prayer on the power of God. The result was that the boy experienced a resurrection. Jesus' actions pointed forward to the time when he would conquer all the powers of darkness—in the weakness of the cross and the triumph of his own Resurrection. At the same time he was laying down the principle of all spiritual service in God's kingdom: God takes the weak things of this world to destroy the influence of the things which are mighty. In this way the glory is always his.

42

Understanding Jesus

Mark 9:30–37

This section in Mark's Gospel, beginning with the confession of Simon Peter at Caesarea Philippi (8:27–30) presents the turning point of Jesus' ministry. From this point onwards, Jesus is on the Via Dolorosa to Jerusalem. Now, in Mark's account, the miraculous becomes rare. The focus of attention is on the cross, and the implications it carries for Jesus' disciples. This explains why Jesus valued privacy so highly (v 30): 'because he was teaching his disciples' that he would soon be crucified in Jerusalem.

The disciples' difficulties

In the course of the narrative, three significant things are said about the disciples.

1. They could not understand Jesus

To us, what he taught them seems plain enough. How could they fail to grasp the fact that he was going to die? But we know now what they did not know. Nothing could have been more repugnant to their minds than to believe what he was telling them. He was saying, quite literally, that he already was betrayed. Although the event had not been accomplished, it was certain. But, since Jesus was still with them, how could they take in that he was already handed over to be crucified?

What was particularly difficult for them to grasp was that Jesus was interpreting the Old Testament Scriptures in a quite different way from the way they had been taught them. He spoke of himself as the 'Son of Man' (v 31). That enigmatic title could simply mean that he was the faithful servant of God (like Ezekiel). But it might also be a reference to the figure described in Daniel 7, who receives honour and glory from 'The Ancient of Days' (see Daniel 7:9–14). Yet, Jesus seemed to identify the destiny of this figure with that of another Old Testament figure—the Suffering Servant of Isaiah 52:13–53:12.

How could the figure of glory (the Son of Man) also be the figure of shame (the Suffering Servant)? They simply could not understand. Only later would they see that it was through his death as Suffering Servant, that he entered into his glory as Son of Man.

We have not rightly understood the identity of Jesus until we have seen that he is both.

2. *They were afraid to ask Jesus*

They did not really understand him. They were afraid to ask him what he meant. Why should that be—since Jesus was surely the most approachable of men? The answer lies in the fact that their Master's repeated stress on his passion underlined just how central it was in his own thinking. Yet they were his disciples, they should have known what his mission was. But the implications were just too enormous for them to accept. It is not really surprising that they hesitated to raise the subject with him.

But there was probably another element which induced fear in their hearts: the seriousness with which

Jesus spoke, and the strength of his commitment to his task. Their own spirits were not really in tune with Jesus' spirit. It frightened them to hear him speak like this, because his commitment was a silent summons to them to share it. But now, as later, they found the message of the cross was a stumbling block. They were not the last disciples to react like that.

3. *They argued about position*

As though to drive home the spiritual weakness of the disciples, Mark records the sad story of their argument.

Mark gives the impression that Jesus had almost been isolated from the disciples after his announcement. No doubt his commitment to the cross showed on his face. It was a time when none of the disciples felt able to walk alongside him.

But Jesus was far more conscious of what the disciples were doing than they had imagined (how foolish they and we can be!). When they were settled in Capernaum he asked a question to which their answer was an embarrassed silence (v 34). They had been arguing about which one of them would be the greatest in the kingdom. Jesus had just spoken about his own forthcoming shameful rejection, but meanwhile the disciples, supposedly his followers, had been arguing about their status.

If we did not know our own hearts we would find it difficult to believe that this really happened. But any disciple who knows himself knows the echoes in his own life of such unfaithfulness.

Jesus once again took time to teach them the principles of the kingdom of God. It is one in which service, not personal kudos, is the central theme. The disciple is recognised not by the honour he gives to those who are important in the world's eyes, but by how he responds to those who possess neither position nor importance—like children. You can almost picture Jesus, just at this point. He called the youngest boy in the home they were in, and bringing him into the middle of the discussion, turned to the disciples and said: 'It is only when you learn to welcome little ones like this that you have really learned to welcome me. And only when you have learned to welcome me, have you welcomed the Father who sent me.'

Jesus spoke in Aramaic. In that language the word for 'child' also serves as the word for 'servant' (rather like the French *garçon*). Was he saying: 'It is only when you learn to receive me as the Servant of the Lord in my acts of humility, that you will really be submitted to God'?

If it is still true today that your attitude to those who have no 'standing' in society, reflects your attitude to the Lord Jesus, what kind of disciple are you?

43

Sons of Thunder

Mark 9:38–42

In three successive chapters of his Gospel, Mark records Jesus' teaching on the reason for his coming. He is going to Jerusalem to die, in order to fulfil the prophecies of Scripture. He is the Suffering Servant of whom Isaiah had spoken. He is the One who will be wounded and bruised for the sins of men.

Shortly after each of these statements, Mark also includes some response on the part of the disciples. Each response shows how little they grasped what their Lord was teaching them. In Mark 8:32, Peter responded in words which reminded Jesus of the temptations he faced in the wilderness at the beginning of his ministry. Later, in Mark 10:35, it was James and John who showed their true colours by seeking advancement in the kingdom of God, instead of exercising commitment to the cross of Christ. Here, it is John on his own.

We know John, affectionately and rightly, as 'the apostle of love'. It is instinctive to think of him in terms of the graciousness of his life. Yet that seems to be far from the real truth about him. For Jesus gave John (and his brother James) the nickname 'Boanerges' (Mk 3:17). Notice that it was Jesus who gave them this name! It means 'sons of thunder'. It hardly indicates that by nature John was meek and gentle. On the contrary, he was a firebrand! In this story we have an illustration of how his fiery zeal was misplaced.

Misplaced zeal

John, and perhaps the other disciples too, had seen someone driving out demons by using the name of Jesus. John's words betray the attitude of his heart towards this man: 'he was not one of us' (v 38). So he had rebuked him and told him to stop. On his return, he reported his diligence to the Master. He had made sure there would be no 'unauthorised use' of Jesus' name!

We can understand John's feelings. We may well have shared them ourselves in other connections. There is nothing more irritating than being official yourself, and discovering that someone else is able to do all you can (and more) but lacks the right qualifications. Perhaps the sting in the tail for John was that just a few days before the other disciples had been powerless to help a man's demon-possessed son. Now, as though to rub salt into the wounds, someone else was casting out demons!

Jesus showed extraordinary restraint and patience with John. He reminded him that ministry in Jesus' name was not the prerogative of the few, but the privilege of all those who belonged to the kingdom. Anyone who shared in the work of that kingdom (as this man was obviously doing) would not 'in the next moment say anything bad about me' (v 39).

Not against Jesus

From this strange incident, Jesus drew an important lesson for his followers; 'Whoever is not against us is for us' (v 40). But what does this mean? Was Jesus taking a laissez-faire attitude to discipleship? Do we not meet people who tell us that they have 'nothing against Christ, personally', yet seem far removed from being his disciples? Is Jesus saying that these too are really on his side?

What had concerned Jesus was that John's response to this man had been totally negative because John's chief interest had been his own exclusive relationship to Christ and his commission from him. He had manifested a deep-seated 'them-and-us' mentality because he was anxious to safeguard his own role. His real concern had not been for Christ's honour and kingdom. So Jesus had explained: 'the real issue is not whether this man is one of your group, John, but whether he is for me or against me.' Later, the apostle Paul would try to introduce a similar principle into the church at Rome: 'Accept one another, then, just as Christ has accepted you, in order to bring praise to God' (Rom 15:7).

Perhaps the reason Jesus was so gentle with John was that John's words were as much a confession as a statement. Did he realise in the light of what Jesus had just said (vv 33–7) that he had done a shameful thing? Was that why Jesus had gently pressed home his point: 'John, even the person who only gives someone a cup of cold water in my name—never mind casts out demons—will not lose his reward'. In the last analysis, it is more important that the servants of God are devoted to Christ than that they are 'one of us'. Indeed, our Lord adds, if we cause one of those who belong to him to sin, we will receive the most terrible of judgements. Better to be thrown into the sea with a stone round your neck than to bring such offence.

Do we really take that seriously? Or do we, however secretly, despise what Jesus says here? Would Jesus give you the same nickname he had given to John—son of thunder? Is that how you are known by other Christians? It is not a compliment!

44

Christianity Is Serious

Mark 9:43–50

In the previous section of this chapter we noticed Jesus warning his disciples not to cause any of his 'little ones' to stumble. It is clear from the context that Jesus did not have children exclusively in mind. All those who serve Christ are in view. If we cause them to sin, we deserve the most severe of judgements. For indifference to those for whom Christ has died is indifference to Christ himself. If he gave his life for them, we belittle him if we belittle them.

The theme of stumbling is continued in the passage which follows; but this time Jesus is warning his disciples against the danger of stumbling themselves by their failure to deal with sin.

Fire of condemnation

Jesus spoke with great seriousness and concreteness about sin. He does not treat it lightly, nor does he offer cheap and easy remedies. On the contrary, only when we aim at the complete eradication of sin are we likely to have any success against its influence. We are faced with two alternatives: kill sin, or sin will eventually kill us.

There can be no reconciliation between the Christian and sin, and no platform for negotiation. If we do not engage in the effort to conquer it, we may be sure that it will conquer us. We must put out the fires of sin in our hearts, or we will find ourselves exposed to the flames of hell and separation from God, permanently (v 48).

It is not an accident that Jesus speaks about sin in relation to the hand, the eye and the foot (vv 43–7). He is not really suggesting that we engage in acts of self-mutilation in order to be free from sin. Rather, he is underlining the fact that sin is not a 'spiritual' reality which has no relation to daily life. On the contrary, we express our sinfulness through what we do with our hands, what we gaze at with our eyes, where we go to on our feet. The Christian gospel, therefore, summons us to present our bodies to the Lord, as offerings of holiness (see Romans 6:13, 19; 12:1–2). The battle for purity is serious, and it is life-long. The alternative to winning that battle is the loss of our whole life, in the flames of condemnation.

Fire of purification

But there is another 'fire' of which Jesus speaks: the fire of purification; 'everyone will be salted with fire' (v 49).

In the Old Testament, the sacrifices made in the temple were seasoned with salt (Lev 2:13). Jesus seems to be saying here that as we offer our lives to Christ, we too will become like those sacrifices. But we will be seasoned with fire, not salt—the trials which will purge away all the dross of our Christian lives so that only those who have taken Christ's summons seriously will remain standing. Perhaps this is the background to what Peter was later to write about the importance of not being surprised by the fiery trial (1 Pet 1:6–7; 4:12). Through it our faith will emerge, tested and purified for Christ's glory.

Salt of consecration

A further 'word association' occurs in verse 50. The mention of being 'salted' (v 49) leads to the 'saltiness' of Christians. We are to have 'salt' in ourselves.

In Jesus' world, of course, salt was a basic commodity essential to life itself. It was said that 'the world cannot survive without salt' because of its value as a food-preservative. What a tragedy, then, if salt were to lose its saltiness.

Our Lord's point is that unless we maintain the purity of our own lives (plucking out the eye, etc) and are purified by the flames of testing, and remain faithful to Christ, our lives will have no preserving influence on this corrupt world. If we begin to fall into the same patterns of life as those which are characteristic of the world, we will never be able to point men and women to another world.

In view of this, Jesus adds, by way of application: 'be at peace with each other' (v 50). Does that seem an anticlimax after his great summons to moral purity? Not at all. It is precisely in the ability of Christians to love one another truly and humbly from the heart that the community of believers is distinguished from the back-biting or back-scratching communities of the world. Being at peace with one another is a reflection of the God-given peace we have first received from Jesus Christ. Jesus never down-played the powerful witness of true Christian fellowship. Neither should we.

Jesus leaves us here with some heart-searching questions: Am I treating sin casually? Am I willing to be cleansed through fiery trials? Am I living the kind of life which will make a real impact on society? Am I really preserving loving relationships with my fellow-Christians?

45
Divorce

Mark 10:1–12

The ministry of Jesus in Galilee had come to an end. He now continued his work in Judea as he prepared for the final journey to Jerusalem and for the suffering he had already predicted he would experience (Mk 9:31). Crowds followed him and listened to his teaching. But with them came the little deputation we have now become accustomed to meeting—'some Pharisees' (v 2).

These men came to 'test' Jesus. Mark uses this verb on four occasions. Three times it refers to the Pharisees (Mk 8:11; 10:2; 12:15). But its first use in the Gospel describes the activity of Satan (Mk 1:13). That is highly significant. Mark means us to ask, 'Where did I see this kind of testing before? Why, it was when Satan tested Jesus in the wilderness!'

Scripture twisting

The parallel stretches beyond the use of the same verb. The Pharisees' activity involved the same mis-handling of Scripture which had characterised Satan's approach to Jesus (see Matthew 4:1–10).

The Pharisees questioned Jesus about the legitimacy

of divorce. It was one of the major debating points among them, and divided them into two schools of thought. One took a relatively easy-going attitude, allowing divorce for almost any reason; the other took a much stricter line. It is interesting to notice what 'sins' really concerned these men.

But Jesus was wise to them. He knew that they would try to gain some 'leverage' out of his reply. He pointed them back to Scripture. Now *he* would put *them* to the test! 'What did Moses command you?' he asked (v 3). Immediately they replied that 'Moses permitted divorce' (v 4). Little did they realise that they had already revealed the inner workings of their hearts, and indicated they were out of tune with the Author of Scripture.

The Pharisees referred to what Moses had said in Deuteronomy 24:1–3, which should be read in this connection. They argued that there Moses gave permission for divorce to take place if a man found something 'indecent' in his wife. The point of debate among the Pharisees was merely over what constituted something 'indecent'.

But this reply neglected the context in which these verses of Scripture were written, and indeed their wider context in the whole word of God. Moses' words were intended to create a legal barrier to men sinning as they pleased. They were meant in part to protect the rights of women. Rather than giving permission for divorce, they were intended to restrict the ease with which divorce would take place. Moses' words reminded men of the solemn vows of commitment taken in marriage. But the Pharisees had twisted this. What was intended to be a barrier against licence, some of the Pharisees had turned into a bridge to easy divorce.

Jesus' interpretation

Jesus recognised that divine laws on divorce had been issued in the Old Testament. But those laws were intended to restrict man's rebellion against God's fundamental law of marriage, given in Genesis 2:24. There marriage was viewed as a life-long and exclusive relationship between one man and one woman. God had not changed his mind about that. The purpose was still the same: a man is united permanently to his wife in marriage (v 8); no man should ever separate them (v 9).

Talk first about marriage

Jesus raised the discussion on to a different plane altogether. The Pharisees wanted to talk about divorce; he insisted on talking about marriage. Their primary interest lay in seeing how far they could go and still remain within the letter of the law. Jesus' primary interest was in restoring men to the lifestyle for which they had been made. In that context one-man–one-woman marriage was not a restriction of liberty, but the sphere of its enjoyment and development. It was a gift from the Father. The reason the Pharisees found this so unpalatable was because their hearts were so hardened against the Father.

The Pharisees may have been stunned by what Jesus said. The disciples certainly were. When they were alone with him they questioned him about his teaching. Asking Jesus questions was admirable. But their questions revealed the extent to which their thinking too had been influenced by their environment. Matthew's account suggests they regarded Jesus' standards as impossible. It would be better not to marry if this were the expectation (Mt 19:10)!

Jesus did not change his stance in order to please his disciples. Indeed, he emphasised that someone who divorces his partner and remarries is committing adultery.

Mark assumes here the teaching found elsewhere in the New Testament that marital unfaithfulness or blatant desertion may end a marriage in any case (Mt 19:9 and 1 Cor 7:15ff). In such circumstances a Christian may act as though his or her spouse were dead (the Old Testament punishment for such marital sin was death, leaving the individual free to remarry). But such exceptions simply recognise the reality of sin, they do not excuse it. Indeed, they underline the deep solemnity of marital sin.

We can almost hear the protests of the disciples echoing across the centuries (they were no different from twentieth-century people, in this respect). Jesus, however, did not waver. He knew that the stability of family and society life depended on the marriage institution being honoured. If this basic creation design were overthrown, moral, spiritual, psychological and social chaos would result.

How devastatingly relevant to the present day these words of Jesus are! How like the disciples some modern Christians have become. But Jesus did not change the Maker's instructions then—nor has he done so since. We should be grateful that he pointed men back to the original design for life in God's kingdom. Only when we follow that design does marriage 'work' as it should. And when a marriage begins to fail, only re-reading, and re-following the Maker's instructions can repair and save it.

46

Children and the Kingdom of God

Mark 10:13–17

Mark has just recorded an incident which revealed the unbiblical thinking of the Pharisees. Now he shares with us another story of narrow hearts. But this time the culprits are the disciples! Jesus had earlier warned them to watchout for 'the yeast of the Pharisees' (Mk 8:15). Here we see one of the reasons why.

Some parents were bringing their children to Jesus for his blessing. Normally they would have brought them to one of the recognised rabbis for that purpose. Jesus seems to have been moved by the fact that these parents wanted him to receive and pray for their children. It was an expression of their recognition of his grace and their trust in him.

Disciples out of line

The disciples, however, were less than impressed and rebuked them (Mark interestingly uses the masculine pronoun, indicating that it was not just mothers who brought their children to Christ!). Young children had no standing in society. Who did these parents think they were, adding to the Master's burdens?

The truth of the matter was that this reflected the attitude of the disciples, not the attitude of Jesus. He was 'indignant' when he saw what was happening (v 14). That is strong language indeed. Jesus, angry with his disciples? Surely that was something to be reserved for the Pharisees? That is exactly why Jesus was so indignant: his disciples were doing the very thing for which he so consistently opposed the Pharisees! They misrepresented the character of God. They distorted his grace and they diluted his holiness. The disciples were now doing the same thing in connection with Jesus. By their actions they were saying 'This is what Jesus is like. He has no time for you or your children!' No wonder their Master was so deeply moved. What to the disciples was an exercise of their authority was to Jesus a complete distortion of the kingdom of God!

NOT A REWARD BUT A GIFT

In this context, Jesus said two things.

1. The kingdom belongs to such

He urged the children to come, or be brought to him, because 'the kingdom of God belongs to such as these' (v 14).

Sometimes this statement has been read as though Jesus had said, 'The characteristics of these children have a spiritual parallel. If that spiritual parallel is present in your life, then the kingdom of God belongs to you'. But that is not what Jesus says in verse 14. It is what he says in the next verse (v 15). In verse 14, Jesus is saying: 'I am the King in the kingdom of God. I belong to these children and all those who are like them.' These children should not be held back from him precisely because Jesus and his kingdom belong to them!

Does this mean that all children belong naturally to

the kingdom of God? That can hardly be the case, for Scripture teaches us that naturally we are the children of wrath, not the children of the kingdom (Eph 2:3). What then did Jesus mean?

Part of the answer lies in identifying those about whom he is speaking. They belonged to parents who were sufficiently committed to Jesus to take their little ones to him in public for his blessing. That blessing was the blessing of the king. As he prayed for them, Jesus asked that they would receive the blessings of the new covenant in his blood.

Did this mean that irrespective of their response to Jesus these children would always belong to the kingdom of God? Many Christians have misunderstood Jesus' words here because they are afraid that is the implication of taking them at their face value. But if we remember the context in which Jesus speaks we will not make that mistake. He is speaking about children whose parents are already disciples (and will in turn 'disciple' them). Such parents know they need to teach their children the responsibilities of kingdom life, as well as the privileges of kingdom possession. If the blessings of God are rejected in disobedience, they are forfeited. Nothing that is said here implies any other position on the part of Jesus.

2. *Receiving the kingdom*

This becomes all the clearer when we notice the general application Jesus draws from this incident: 'any-one who will not receive the kingdom of God like a little child will never enter it' (v 15).

Sometimes these words are also misunderstood, as though Jesus meant we must be willing, submissive and generally angelic if we are to enter the kingdom! But quite apart from being a strange reflection on the ways of children, that would be to teach that certain qualities qualify us for salvation in God's kingdom! That would be a denial of the gospel.

Children had no standing in Jesus' society. If they were to receive anything it could not be on the basis of their present rights, but only as a gift. Similarly, if any of us is to receive the kingdom of God it must be as a completely unmerited gift from God. If we do not receive the kingdom that way, 'like a little child' (v 15) it will never belong to us.

The thrust of Jesus' words about the kingdom belonging to children is this: the kingdom of God is a gift, not a right. It is given by grace, not earned by qualifications. Christ gives it as he chooses. He had chosen to give it to these children, who were brought in faith by their parents.

No wonder he was indignant with the disciples. They were in danger of turning the gospel of the gift of the kingdom into a Pharisaic message about earning the kingdom.

In our concern to emphasise our responsibility to repent and believe, we must never make the mistake of the Pharisees—or the disciples. We do not need to 'guard' the grace of God (as the Pharisees and the disciples here tried to do). It will guard itself by the new life it produces in us.

47

Rich, but Sad

Mark 10:17–31

Jesus had been speaking about receiving the kingdom of God as a little child. While his words were still clearly embedded in his disciples' memories an incident occurred which vividly illustrated what he had taught them. A young man ran up to him and asked him on bended knee what he needed to do in order to have eternal life. Luke's Gospel underlines just how remarkable this was by telling us the man was a 'ruler' (ie in the local synagogue, Luke 18:18). Here, surely, was a wonderful opportunity for Jesus to establish a beachhead in a whole community by making this respected young man one of his disciples!

But Jesus never pursued slick and easy methods of evangelism. In fact, the disciples must have thought his initial response to this man was frankly disappointing! He began to discuss theology with him! With apparent respect, this young enquirer had addressed Jesus as 'Good teacher' (v 18). Jesus' curious reply was to ask him why he had called him 'good' since no one was good except God!

Only as we follow through the conversation between them does Jesus' response to the rich young man begin to make sense. He had asked Jesus about eternal life in God's kingdom. Painstakingly, Jesus led him, and later his own disciples, through a series of lessons which were (and are) vital for all who would enter into eternal life.

ETERNAL LIFE!

1. Knowledge of God

Later, in his great prayer in John 17, Jesus distilled the essence of eternal life. It is to 'know you, the only true God, and Jesus Christ, whom you have sent' (Jn 17:3). Eternal life means knowing the Father and the Son. It means knowing the Father through the Son, because the Son is equal with the Father and is the One who makes him known (Jn 1:1–2,18).

When Jesus said, 'Why do you call me good, when we both know that God alone is good? (v 18), he was pressing home the question: 'Do you really know God? Your words suggest that you see an intimate relationship between God and Myself. Do you really see that?'

2. Knowledge of ourselves

This is the point of Jesus' apparently casual reference to the Law of Moses (v 19). Already he had taken the measure of the man. That is probably why the commandments he refers to would test whether his understanding of the Law was outward and merely formal, or inward and spiritual. Would the young man see that these commandments revealed sinful motives as well as sinful actions (see Matthew 5:21–48)? Would he see that Jesus had said nothing about his relationship to the living God—that this question was only 'for openers'?

The young man revealed the sad superficiality of his self-understanding. He volunteered the information that he had kept these commandments from boyhood. He was like Paul before the full force of the Law showed him the real nature of his heart. He thought he was alive, when in fact he was spiritually dead (Rom 7:9). 'As for legalistic righteousness' he too was 'faultless' (Phil 3:6). But he was blind to what he was really like inside.

JESUS LOVED HIM, BUT . . .

Do not think for a moment that this young man was a rogue. The reverse was the case. He was an earnest, sincere, religious, devoted young man. As far as he understood his own heart he had kept the commandments. In every human respect he was the kind of man most of us secretly admire, but fail to imitate. That was why Jesus 'looked at him and loved him' (v 21). But something was missing—one thing which amounted to everything. His life was still centred on himself rather than on the kingdom of God.

With a surgeon-like cut, Jesus expertly, and unexpectedly, exposed the man's need: 'Go, sell your possessions, give everything to the poor, and then come and follow me. You will then have treasure in heaven' (v 21).

One sentence was enough to teach this young man the truth about himself that had been hidden all these years. He had outwardly kept the commandments; but there was a god in his life which he prized more than the knowledge of the true God: 'he had great wealth' (v 22). Sadly, with his heart deception now unveiled, he turned round and went back to the idol worship from which he had almost escaped. Only, now he knew the truth about himself.

Here was a man who had great wealth, and was not willing to take the 'risk' of faith, by leaving it for the sake of greater wealth. What was his mistake? He made his greatest ever decision on the basis of this life rather than on the basis of eternal life. If only he had remembered the story of Moses which must have been read to him so often 'from boyhood'! He counted 'disgrace for the sake of Christ as of greater value than the treasures of Egypt, because he was looking ahead to his reward' (Heb 11:26). Moses calculated on the basis of eternal arithmetic. This young man relied on the inaccurate calculator he had always used: wealth. He stands as a perpetual monument to the fact that if we have everything, but have not Christ, we ultimately have nothing. The special tragedy of his life—as he made his way home sadly—was that now he knew it.

48

All for Jesus

Mark 10:23–31

The whole of Jesus' attention had been given to the rich ruler who had come to him seeking eternal life. Now, as the young man turned away sadly, clinging to his possessions rather than responding to Christ's invitation, Jesus turned to his disciples. There must have been sadness in his eyes and on his face. There was certainly deep sadness in his words, as he commented on what they had all witnessed: 'How hard it is for the rich to enter the kingdom of God!' (v 23).

Needles and camels

His words astonished the disciples—despite all they had just seen. After all, the rich had many advantages. From a human point of view it seemed to be so much easier for them to live lives which pleased God. They did not have the fears and anxieties which the poor knew; they had time on their hands to spend in religious learning and actions ('idle rich' doubtless some of the disciples would say).

The disciples had still not learned the real meaning of the conversation between Jesus and the young man. So their Lord underlined it for them with one of his most memorable sayings: It is as difficult for the rich to enter God's kingdom as it is for a camel to go through the eye of a needle!

Various efforts have been made to find the source of this statement—was there a city gate somewhere in Jesus' time known as 'The Needle's Eye' through which camels came and were unloaded in order to enter? Is this some kind of well-known proverbial saying? But the source of the illustration is far less important than its message. Jesus is saying, in the most vivid fashion possible, that in terms of natural ability it is utterly impossible for a rich man to enter the kingdom of God!

Can anyone be saved?

The response of the twelve was open-mouthed incredulity. If this were so, surely nobody could be saved! That was probably the response Jesus expected. Having already taught the disciples (in his conversation with the ruler) the significance of the true knowledge of God and the knowledge of self, he now wanted to show them the knowledge of God's grace. What man could never do, God alone can do (v 27).

What did Jesus mean? He meant that eternal life not only has God as its goal, it has God as its source and beginning. Only he can give it! Only when he gives us new hearts, to abandon everything for Christ, will we be free from our personal forms of idolatry and yield to the principles of the divine kingdom (Ezek 36:25–7). The message of the encounter with the Rich Young Ruler in Mark's Gospel teaches the same lessons as Jesus' encounter with Nicodemus in John's Gospel (3:1ff). Eternal life, the kingdom of God, salvation—these can only be ours when we are cast on the mercy and grace of God to give them to us.

Leave everything

Significantly, it is Simon Peter who blurts out what was on the minds of most of the disciples: 'We have left everything to follow you!' (v 28).

Did Peter never get his sentence finished? Was he going to ask a question about where they stood? He did not need to. Jesus understood his consternation of mind. He knew that even for his own disciples the radical challenge he had just issued must have brought deep self-questioning about their own level of commitment to him. We can almost hear Peter saying, 'Lord, we're not rich men; we have not left such treasures; but, Lord, we have left everything we had!'

Our Lord's response contains some of the greatest words of encouragement to be found anywhere in Scripture. Yes, he recognises that to follow him will involve many in suffering persecution (v 30). But will that 'sacrifice' involve 'loss'? By no means. Jesus promises that whatever his disciples sacrifice for his sake and for the spread of the gospel will be given back to them 'a hundred times as much in this present age...and in the age to come, eternal life' (v 30).

Multiplication, not subtraction!

It is a staggering promise, and, to a casual reader of the Gospels, an impossible one. We can understand 'pie in the sky when you die' ('in the age to come, eternal life!'), but 'pie now'? That is what Jesus seems to be promising.

From outside the kingdom, where the reality of its power is an unknown quantity, the promise appears ludicrous. Yet thousands, millions of Christians throughout the ages could testify how this promise has come true in their lives. Christ has never been their debtor. He has supplied all their needs. Even when becoming a Christian has meant leaving family, or being rejected by them—

Christ has given back a hundred families to his servants. It is one of the most stubborn facts of history that this promise has been fulfilled. Christ, as David Livingstone once said, was a gentleman, and has kept his word.

This was something the rich young ruler never discovered, as far as we know. It is one of the 'secrets of the kingdom of God'. Is it one on which you have ventured everything?

49

Towards Jerusalem

Mark 10:32–45

Chapters 8, 9 and 10 of Mark's Gospel are punctuated by Jesus' three-fold announcement of his impending suffering and death (8:31–2; 9:31; 10:33). There is a growing sense in the narrative that Jesus is steadily making his way to fulfil his destiny. Mark pictures Jesus striding out in front of his disciples and those who accompanied them. There was 'something about him' now that had a profound effect on them all. It was not that he had resolved something which had been troubling him. It was more a sense of almost frightening determination in his whole bearing. The disciples (who must have assumed by this time that they knew Jesus 'inside out') were 'astonished'; the others who were with them were 'afraid' (v 32). The degree of commitment which Jesus manifested was something they had never encountered before. They could not fully understand it; but it unnerved them just because it drew them into its own orbit. They sensed that his commitment required their commitment!

Detailed prophecy

Taking the disciples aside, Jesus explained his mission in greater detail than before. They were going to Jerusalem—and Jerusalem was where he would die! He, the Messiah, would be treated with contempt by his own people. They would hand their own promised Messiah over to the Gentiles to be mocked and spat upon, flogged and eventually executed (v 33–4).

Now his followers were in possession of almost all of the details which would be fulfilled so soon. How did they react?

On similar occasions they had reacted very badly. As Mark records their 'spiritual pulse rate' in response to these revelations of Jesus, it had been very poor. On the first occasion Peter had tried to divert Jesus; on the second, the disciples had begun to argue about which one of them was the greatest. By now, however, they would surely have learned their lesson.

Selfish requests

Sadly, they had not. As the journey continued, James and John realised the significance of what they had just heard. Their Messiah was going to suffer in Jerusalem, and then he was going to rise again! This could mean only one thing: the Messianic Age, promised in the Old Testament Scriptures, was almost here. The Messianic banquet would soon be served. Now was the time to stake their claim for a place of honour in the coming world, beside Jesus himself! It may well be that these brothers had usually found themselves in the places of honour when the disciples ate together—some people seem to have a knack of always being next to the central character!

Jesus immediately took them to task. They did not really understand what they were asking. Nor did they understand how insensitive their selfishness was in the light of what Jesus was about to do. Like Peter before them, they were looking for a crown without a cross, glory without suffering, honour without humility.

The wine and the water

This is the point of the question Jesus asked them: 'You cannot drink of my cup and be baptised with my baptism, can you?' (v 38, where the question is phrased in such a way as to expect 'no' as the answer). On the cross, Jesus would drink the cup of God's wrath against sin, he would be baptised (or overwhelmed) with the waters of God's wrath! But the brothers were undeterred—what did Jesus know about what they could and could not do? Yes, they could share both his cup and his baptism. They did not pause to reflect on the meaning of either.

With a hint of sadness, Jesus assured the disciples that they would indeed drink a cup and receive a baptism of suffering. But it was the prerogative of his Father, not his own, to bestow the places of honour at the Messianic Banquet. Did they not yet understand? Had they not learned yet to imitate him, and seek honour for the Father rather than for themselves?

Chain reaction

When the others heard what had happened—perhaps from the two sheepish brothers reporting their conversation with Jesus—they proved themselves to be no better. They were furious. Their own pride was hurt. It was time for Jesus to step in once more to underline the principle they had so badly failed to keep.

What was that principle? It was very simple. The way of the disciple is different from the way of the world. In the kingdom of God, true greatness is measured by our service, not by the number of our servants. It is seen, not in how high up the ladder we have climbed, but how far down the ladder we are prepared to climb for the sake of others. True discipleship has at its heart letting go of our desire for honour in this world, in order to bestow honour on others.

But discipleship is also a 'modelling' process. It means being like Jesus! He came to serve others, not to be served by them. He came to give his life for others. If James and John and all the others really were going to be his disciples, then it was time they began to live like their Master.

The 'simple' words of Jesus are always the most difficult, aren't they?

50

A Blind Beggar

Mark 10:46–52

Passover was approaching. It was time for pilgrimages to Jerusalem for the annual feast. What this meant to the Old Testament believer is recorded in the fifteen 'Songs of Ascents' (Psalms 120–134). They perfectly expressed the wide variety of spiritual experience involved in travelling there. No doubt some of those Psalms were sung on the way, as pilgrims lifted up their eyes to the hills, contemplated the danger of their journey (especially on the road between Jericho and Jerusalem—see Luke 11:30!) and as they arrived in the city (see Psalms 121, 122).

Jesus was in the middle of such a crowd of pilgrims. They were now in Jericho (v 46). It was here, just outside the city gate, that Jesus met Bartimaeus, the man whose blindness condemned him to a world of darkness and poverty, and reduced him to beggarhood.

Bartimaeus

We do not know how Bartimaeus had heard about Jesus. It seems likely that Jesus' name was on the lips of many of the pilgrims as they talked together. The stories of his teaching and healing must have figured prominently. Had Bartimaeus put two and two together, in order to conclude that this Man was no ordinary teacher or healer? Had he heard how Jesus claimed to be the One on whom the Spirit of the Lord had been promised to rest, who would give sight to the blind (Lk 4:18)?

As he heard the crowds passing by, Bartimaeus learned that Jesus was with them. This might well be the only opportunity he would ever have. At the top of his voice he shouted out, 'Son of David, have mercy on me!' (v 48).

Naturally the crowd told him to hold his tongue (wouldn't you have done the same?). They were there for the spectacle of seeing Jesus on his way to Jerusalem. Many of them must have realised that a confrontation of monumental proportions might result. Bartimaeus had only nuisance value under such circumstances.

The blind beggar cried out all the more. Nothing would stop him. Jesus heard him. He stopped, and called him.

Was it the same people who had sought to silence him who now told him to 'cheer up'? Did their words indicate a sadness in Bartimaeus' cry which now touched their hearts? Or were they interested only in the 'sport' of the occasion? Mark gives us no answer. His attention is now completely focused on the encounter between Jesus and Bartimaeus.

Why call on Jesus?

Jesus' question perhaps appears naive: 'What do you want me to do?' (v 51). But its simplicity is deceptive. It went straight to the heart of the matter. Why had Bartimaeus called on Jesus? Did he need financial assistance? What did he really want? He answered immediately. There was only one thing he wanted from Jesus: his sight. His request for it was the evidence that he believed Jesus could provide it. And he did. Bartimaeus could see immediately. And, says Mark, 'he followed Jesus along the road' (v 52). What a scene that must have been!

The Gospel in action

This is the penultimate miracle in Mark's Gospel, a further visual presentation of the presence of the kingdom of God. It gathers together several important lessons.

No miracle in this Gospel more vividly illustrates the promise God had given through the prophet Joel. When God establishes his kingdom 'everyone who calls on the name of the Lord will be saved' (Joel 2:32). Bartimaeus encountered Jesus' power, not on the basis of his strength, but in the context of his weakness. The crowd around him believed (rightly) that he had nothing he could contribute to what Jesus was doing. They did not understand that this was not a disqualification from calling on the Lord's name (in effect, it was they, and not Bartimaeus, who were blind). Bartimaeus brought nothing but his need. But in doing so he fulfilled a fundamental law in God's kingdom: there is no other way to come to Jesus but on the basis of our need and his adequacy to meet it fully.

Jesus had time

A further element emerges in this story. Jesus had time for Bartimaeus. When we recall the context—the sense of fear in the disciples' hearts as they watched Jesus go to Jerusalem with such awe-inspiring determination—our Lord's tender care for one blind beggar is profoundly moving. His willingness to stop, when his own heart must have been heavy with sorrow; his concern that Bartimaeus should share his need, when not even his own disciples seemed capable of sharing his own need—all this emphasises the gracious character of the Saviour. It stands also in marked contrast to the events of the previous section, when the disciples had fought among themselves for the places of honour and Jesus reminded them that true greatness lies in humble service. If that is so, then Jesus' greatness never stood out more clearly than when he called this helpless man out of his darkness and into the light of a new and more glorious day.

Throughout Mark's Gospel there is an underlying message for the church in Rome, and for the church in all ages. Jesus has not changed, he is still the same. He still stops for those who call on his name, and he listens to our prayers for help.

51

Ride On in Majesty

Mark 11:1–11

Every schoolboy is supposed to know Julius Caesar's famous words before he crossed the River Rubicon, 'The die is cast'. It means that a point of no return has been reached. That was true now of Jesus. He had committed himself to going to Jerusalem. There was no turning back. Now his last days had arrived; the climactic activity of his life was about to begin.

Jesus knew that in the purposes of God he had already been handed over to be shamefully treated and crucified. He must have been conscious that the plotting of his death had been going on now for months (Mk 3:6). But he did not go to the cross as a helpless victim. All the Gospel writers emphasise that Jesus was the Lord and Master both of his disciples and of his own situation. It would be no accident that he would be arrested and crucified. In fact, those events were but further steps in fulfilling his own saving purposes. His majesty and authority begin to shine through from the moment of his entry into Jerusalem.

It seems likely that Jesus' commandeering of the colt was a prearranged action. Perhaps its owner was now with Jesus, so that his servants and neighbours would not think it strange for the animal to be taken to him for Jesus.

KINGLY ARRIVAL

But why did Jesus *ride* into Jerusalem? It was a more unusual act than we might at first think, because pilgrims usually made the last part of their journey to the city on foot. Nor is the explanation simply that he was tired from his journey (although he may well have been). No, his action was one of prophetic symbolism. It was the fulfilment of an ancient prophecy from Zechariah 9:9: 'Rejoice greatly, O daughter of Zion... See, your king comes to you, righteous and having salvation, gentle and riding on a donkey, on a colt, the foal of a donkey.' This was no spur of the moment idea on Jesus' part. For those who had eyes to see, it was a deliberate claim to be the One of whom the prophets had so clearly written.

The crowds of pilgrims who were also making their way to Jerusalem were caught up in what was happening, and began to sing and shout the words of some of the great pilgrim hymns of the psalter. They greeted him as one who had come in the name of the Lord. Cloaks and branches were strewn on the road as the joy of the crowd began to overflow into activity. Doubtless none of them knew that the animal on which Jesus sat had never been ridden before (v 2). But some of the disciples knew—and knew also that the animals used in the Old Testament system of worship were invariably those which had not been employed in secular business. Hidden in the very heart of this symbolism was the message that Jesus had come to give his life as a ransom sacrifice for men's sins!

Humble bearing

Yet, for all Jesus' kingly bearing in his entry into Jerusalem, there is something else we should notice. He does not enter Jerusalem in pomp and circumstance. It is with meekness and lowliness that he enters the city which is to reject him.

These are virtually the only qualities in his own character to which Jesus ever drew attention. In the famous 'comfortable words' he invites us to come to him precisely because he is meek and lowly in heart (Mt 11:28–30). The same qualities had become visible in Jesus' life when, catching sight of the city of Jerusalem, his heart had burst with sorrow and his eyes had filled with tears. He wept over its sin and unbelief (Lk 19:41–4). What a strange way for the Son of David to return to the seat of David's kingdom! Yet there never was a more regal entry into Jerusalem than on that day.

The true victor's triumph

Think, for a moment, what Mark's record would convey to those who read it first—the Christians in Rome. No doubt many of them had seen generals enter Rome in triumph and receive the accolades of victory. How stark the contrast between Roman glory and Jesus' humility must have seemed. How mighty and powerful the sword and political power by contrast with King Jesus! Yet we know that his kingdom was established, while the glory that was Rome disappeared into oblivion. We knew that what Jesus did in Jerusalem established a kingdom which would outlast all the kingdoms of this world and break in pieces every man-centred kingdom which sets itself against it. Jesus had come to take his throne—but had committed himself to begin his reign from a cross.

What were Jesus' thoughts as he made his way to the

temple that evening, and 'looked around at everything' (v 11)? Did he remember the first time he had seen it, as a twelve-year-old boy (Lk 2:41–52)? Did he think back through the history of his people, and ponder some of the statements of the Psalms, about this place where God had made himself known? The Temple had been destroyed before. In a day or two he would tell his disciples that it would soon be destroyed again. There was only one kingdom which would stand—the kingdom which would come soon, through his death and Resurrection. With those thoughts, or similar ones in his mind, he realised it was late, and returned to Bethany. Now it was just a matter of time!

52

Prophet, Priest and King

Mark 11:12–33

Throughout Mark's Gospel, Jesus is always in complete control of every situation. Everything he does is stamped with the imprint of his gracious authority. In the previous section we noted how Jesus rode into Jerusalem as the prophesied king. Yet he came in meekness and lowliness, not in pomp and ostentation. But, that meekness should not be misunderstood as weakness. Jesus entered Jerusalem as the promised Messiah. It is not surprising then that his actions revealed his authority as the prophet, priest and king whom God had sent.

PROPHET

He shows his authority as the prophet whom God has sent by the power of his word. When he spoke to the fig tree (v 14), his word came true (v 20–1). He was hungry. The tree showed signs of bearing fruit—even though it was out of season. But when Jesus went to take the figs promised by the leaves, there were none. He spoke a word of judgement on the tree: no one would ever eat its fruit again. The next morning, as the disciples returned to Jerusalem, they saw the tree withered from its roots.

Was this an act of callous and spiteful malice on Jesus' part? In view of Mark's concern to show Jesus' regal grace, that is unthinkable. Rather, Mark saw in Jesus' action an acted prophecy. Israel, like the fig tree, showed the outward signs of bearing fruit, but those who approached it spiritually hungry found none. Although planted by God, and nurtured by his servants, the people of God were spiritually barren. Like vine branches which bore no fruit, they would be cast aside (Jn 15:6).

Many readers have been alarmed by this action of Jesus. It seems so severe. But it drives us to one of two conclusions: either Jesus was callous and cynical in his use of power, or the question of our spiritual fruitfulness is one of immense seriousness which we ignore at our peril. The Jewish people did ignore it, and within years were exposed to the withering judgement of God. How much we need to learn that, without exception, Jesus means what he says!

Priest

When Jesus arrived at the temple, he demonstrated his authority there as God's priest. The temple had apparently been turned into a market-place, where dishonest commercial exploitation was taking place. Had the priests any sense of dignity or authority they would have cleansed God's sanctuary long before. But it took the God-appointed priest to drive out those who were desecrating the house of God. It was meant to be 'a house of prayer for all nations' (v 17 cf Is 56:7); it had become a commercial market-place instead. Where God's name was to be praised it had been dishonoured and besmirched. That was something Jesus would not tolerate, even if, humanly speaking, it would cost him his life—as indeed it did (v 18).

There are few more awe-inspiring passages in Scripture than this one. Here Jesus' holy wrath burned with frightening purity. Single-handed, he restored the place to its original purpose. As the true priest in the temple of God, he cleansed it for prayer.

Jesus is still the one priest in the church of God. His actions then must make us ask whether the church has learned its lesson yet. What blasphemy when the impression left by the church is that buying and selling in this world and its goods is its chief interest! We should not think that his careful scrutiny of the church is a thing of the past. Think of the postscripts to the seven churches in Asia, appended to John's letter in Revelation 1. There Jesus is pictured again robed in his priestly garments (Rev 1:12–16), scrutinising his temple, urging repentance before it is too late. He comes seeking spiritual fruit and true worship. Is that what is most noticeable about your life and that of your Christian fellowship?

King

The final incident in the chapter records an incident in which Jesus' bearing as king is underlined. He was asked a 'trick question', in the hope that he would condemn himself out of his own mouth (v 28): On whose authority did he act?

Jesus answered with a question of his own (we would do well to learn from him how to respond to cynical opponents of the gospel!). If the priests, lawyers and elders would answer his question, he would in turn answer their question. In fact, as they all knew, the right answer to his question provided the right answer to their question! 'Was John's baptism from heaven, or merely from men?' (v 30).

If they replied 'from men', the religious leaders knew they would face an uprising against them, for John was regarded as a true prophet and martyr—with good reason. But, if they replied 'from God (heaven)' their failure to respond to his ministry would be inexcusable. Not only so, but Jesus himself had been recognised and baptised by John as the Messiah! To acknowledge that John's baptism was God-ordained would be to confess that Jesus was the Christ!

How pathetic these great theologians and leaders must have looked, as they said to Jesus: 'We don't know'! 'Then, you are incapable of recognising the source of my authority' said Jesus (v 33).

What is the lesson? You will not truly confess Jesus as the Christ until you are willing to bow to his authority as your Saviour, Lord and Teacher.

53

The Owner's Son

Mark 12:1–12

Jesus' authority had been demonstrated by his kingly entrance into Jerusalem, and challenged by the religious leaders as they had continued to question him. They had tried to assert their authority over him, but they could not compare with him morally, nor could they hold a candle to him theologically! In argument he was their Master! All their attempts to 'corner' him so far had fallen to the ground. But now Jesus brings the issue to a head himself, by telling a parable which so touched the consciences of the religious leaders that they felt 'he had spoken the parable against them' (v 12). Despite all their deep-seated opposition against him, they were constrained by Jesus' authority to recognise that he was their Master and judge.

Rebellious tenants

Not all of Jesus' parables were so readily understood by his hearers. But they immediately recognised in this one an allusion to the picture of Israel which Isaiah had drawn—as the vineyard of the Lord (Is 5:1–7). Jesus married that to the daily experience of tenant farmers who laboured on the land of absent landlords. In the parable, the tenants were the religious leaders from whom spiritual fruit was expected (v 2). The parable of the vineyard was, in fact, the spoken form of the parable of the fig-tree which Jesus had 'told' in the previous chapter.

The story which Jesus told moved beyond daily experience. Revolts by tenant farmers were not unusual. What would have been unusual was the fact that the owner in Jesus' parable sent servant after servant (vv 2–5). Doubtless the religious leaders realised that the servants in the parable represented the prophets of the Old Testament. The final messenger was the owner's son. There was no doubting his identity. It was Jesus. He was now confronting them, in this semi-veiled manner, with the fact that he knew what their plan was: they intended to destroy him (v 7)! Only their fear of men held them back (v 12).

Notice again how Jesus controls the situation, and is Master of every moment of his own life. Until this time he had carefully avoided unnecessary confrontation with the leaders. But now his time had almost come. He knew that he could issue these warnings and expose these wicked men, and yet still keep to God's timetable. He knew that this would not lead to his immediate or premature death, for one reason: these men lacked the courage of their convictions. Unlike Jesus, they were not prepared to die for their cause, and therefore out of fear of the crowd, they refrained from any action. They lacked 'moral courage'. But, then, how could such men have any?

Reactions

When God's word searches out men's motives and exposes their hearts, two reactions are always possible. Men may see themselves as they really are, repent from their sin, and turn to the Lord. We might think that would be the inevitable response to Jesus' own preaching.

But another kind of response is possible: we can harden our hearts against the one who exposes our need, and resolve with unmitigated bitterness to be rid of his influence. This was the pathway these Jews chose (see verses 7–9). Foolishly they thought they could emerge unscathed. But time proved Jesus right: the vineyard of God was given to others.

Discarded stone fits!

Jesus drew on Psalm 118:22–3 to paint the same picture in different colours. The psalm tells of one of the stones which had been brought to the building site for Solomon's Temple. The stone was discarded as unfit for the sanctuary. Yet, those who rejected it did not realise that it was perfectly shaped and hued to be the capstone of the porch! The stone which the expert builders had rejected was the one which would hold everything together! Jesus, who would be despised and rejected by these leaders was actually essential for access into God's presence! This is God's way. Through what man counts as foolish, God shows that his folly is wiser than the wisdom of men, and his weakness stronger than the strength of men (1 Cor 1:25).

Application

But the lesson of this parable cannot be confined to the religious leaders of Jesus' time. Paul explains that it applies to the church today (which is largely Gentile): branches were broken off so that we could be grafted into God's vine, the church. But while that is true, we must remember God's righteous judgement! Do not be proud and self-sufficient. Rather bow in reverent fear, for if God did not spare the natural branches, will he spare the grafted branches if they eventually show the same hardness of heart (see Romans 11:19–21)? By no means!

God continues to send servants to us, to remind us of our debt to him. In a multitude of ways he reminds us that he looks for the fruit of grace in our lives. His servants may be preachers and teachers of his word; they may be those who remind us personally that we are to live for Christ; they may be the joys and sorrows of life, which encourage us to seek our only ultimate joy and strength in God and his grace. The question is: How do you respond to the messengers God sends? Do you welcome them, or do you seek to silence the voice of God in them?

54

The Opposition United

Mark 12:13–17

Jesus unites people together. He took the unformed clay of young men's lives and shaped them into a band of apostles who were eventually willing to live and die for him. But men are not always united by Jesus in that way. They can also be united in hostility towards him, even if otherwise they have little in common. This was the case with the Pharisees and the Herodians. Mark records that they were in league against him throughout almost the entire period of Jesus' public ministry (Mk 3:6). Together they plotted and schemed his destruction.

Enemies united

Nowhere is this more evident than in the series of 'trick questions' with which Jesus was now faced. Here, the Pharisees, who stood for the old ways, and many of whom were 'hard-liners'; and the Herodians, whose life-style was one of constant compromise rather than principle, forced themselves on Jesus once more. There was one person significant enough to bring them together—Jesus—but it was in sworn opposition to all that he taught and did. Sinking their differences, they were united in opposition to him, just as Herod and Pontius Pilate would be at the end of this week (see Luke 23:1–12).

That was not a phenomenon limited to the first century. In every age, indeed in the experience of every Christian, the time comes when opposites will be reconciled against the gospel. The struggle for the survival of self-centred living will see to that!

Forked tongues

The delegation came with a carefully thought out and pointed trick question. They reminded Jesus of his integrity (speaking, as the Red Indians in the old Western movies used to say 'with forked tongue'). In the light of his known impartiality, faithfulness and teaching ability, they had a question for him. But no sooner were these flattering words out of their mouths than they began to spew out the poisonous venom in their hearts: 'Is it right to pay taxes to Caesar or not?'.

There are several important features in this question. First of all it made room for only two answers: yes and no. Any other answer would seem to avoid the real issue. But, secondly, it was politically loaded. If Jesus answered 'yes', he would take the side of the Pharisees and Herodians, but they knew he would be setting himself against the profound popular hatred of the Roman taxation system. Taxes served as a constant reminder to the Jews that they were a broken and subjugated people. That was why the Zealots' refusal to pay them was regarded as an essential element in nationalistic loyalty. But, then, if Jesus answered 'no, it is wrong to pay taxes to Caesar', he would immediately be accused of treason. He was in a 'no-win' situation—at least the Pharisees and Herodians thought so.

Satanic collusion

Jesus' initial response is significant: 'Why are you trying to trap me?' he asked (v 15). The verb Mark uses to translate Jesus' original statement (which would have been made in his native tongue of Aramaic) is used in the Gospel several times of the Pharisees. But the first time it occurs, it is used of Satan testing Jesus in the wilderness (Mk 1:13). It seems likely that the connection in vocabulary is deliberate on Mark's part: Jesus associated these testings with the efforts of Satan to stand in his way. But, as the rest of the passage shows, our Lord mastered his opponents as successfully as he had earlier overcome Satan in the desert.

Masterly reply

Jesus asked for a coin. The drama in his action is obvious. One can almost hear the crowd around him holding their breath, and a look of puzzlement beginning to come over the faces of his opponents as he asked his question: 'Whose image appears on the Roman coinage?' The answer, of course, was 'Caesar's'.

So what? Jesus responded with devastating simplicity: 'If this coin has Caesar's image on it, then it belongs to him—give him his due'.

Was he giving in to the Pharisees and Herodians so easily? On the contrary. Doubtless the hearts of his enemies began to dance with glee that they had at last cornered him, and forced him to 'save his skin' by compromising with the occupying forces. 'But' Jesus added, 'there is another "coin" I see, bearing a different image—the image of God, stamped on the lives of his creatures. So, I conclude, you must give to God what belongs to him—the whole of your lives'.

With one sentence Jesus exposed the truth about his enemies and demolished their efforts to trick him. He put the question of living under Caesar in its proper place: a distant second behind the more important question of living in the kingdom of God. The man who is devoted to God does not make the issue of his political freedom the number-one priority in his life. He knows that he can serve God, freely in his heart, under the most oppressive of regimes. The fact that these men were hounding Jesus to death demonstrated how far they were from doing that. Exposed, defeated and humiliated, they could only crawl away to regroup on another occasion.

It makes you wonder if an enormous cheer went up from the crowd for Jesus, doesn't it? Certainly this is a passage which makes every disciple thrill with admiration for his Saviour.

55

Question and Answer

Mark 12:18–27

In human warfare through the centuries a major tactic has been to attack the enemy in waves, striking at him before he has the opportunity to recover his defences. The same kind of assault is characteristic of spiritual warfare. In this part of his Gospel, Mark vividly describes how Jesus himself was the object of such attacks, as wave upon wave of 'delegations' came to question him. In Mark 11:27 it had been the chief priests, the teachers of the law and the elders; in Mark 12:13 it had been the Pharisees and the Herodians. Now it was the Sadducees.

The Sadducees

Many of Mark's readers probably knew very little about the internal struggles of the Jewish faith. To them a Jew was a Jew. Distinguishing the various nuances of Jewish religion was uncommon—as it still is today among non-Jews. It is necessary to know at least one thing about the difference between the Pharisees and the Sadducees, however, to understand this incident: Sadducees based their theology on the first five books of the Old Testament, and in particular they denied the doctrine of the resurrection. The question they asked Jesus has this background.

Another element in Old Testament teaching forms the background to their question. In Deuteronomy 25: 5–10 (a section of the Old Testament which the Sadducees did accept as divinely inspired), God had made provision for a family to be raised up for a husband who had died childless. A near relative would marry his widow, and the first child would be counted as the dead man's. In this way the man's name and honour would not be lost. An example of this (called the Levirate law) can be found in the story of Ruth.

Trick question

The Sadducees' trick question was this: Suppose a situation arose where a married man died before his wife had a child, and his brother married her, but he also died childless...and so on, until all seven brothers had married the woman, and had all died childless...whose wife would she be in the resurrection?

This kind of argument is known technically by the Latin phrase *reductio ad absurdum*. It tries to show that some basic belief cannot be true because its implications seem absurd or ridiculous. No doubt there was a good measure of chortling and winking as Jesus was asked the question. For this hypothetical (but, of course, possible!) story seemed to indicate that if God had given the Levirate law (which all agreed he had), it would be ridiculous to believe in the resurrection—just look at what might happen. So, the Sadducees were arguing, the doctrine of the resurrection is impossible.

Doubtless their question was an 'old chestnut'—the kind of question every Sadducee's son asked every Pharisee's son in primary school! No one had ever found an answer to it, and the Sadducees expected no one would.

That is, until they encountered Jesus and foolishly tried to trick him.

Direct speech

What did Jesus say? Notice his reply, step by step.

1. The Sadducees were wrong

Jesus speaks with prophetic brevity. Men who deny the resurrection are simply in error. As far as he was concerned certain things are non-negotiable. This is one of them. We conclude from this that all modern-day Sadducees who profess the Christian tradition but deny the resurrection are opposed to the teaching of Jesus.

2. Behind this error lies ignorance

The Sadducees did not know the word of God or the power of God. They did not understand the many testimonies in the Old Testament to the resurrection. They had so small a view of God that they seemed to think the world to come would be simply a continuation of the world as it is. If they had known the power of God to transform human life, they would have already known what Jesus was about to tell them.

3. Jesus expounded Scripture to prove his point

Pointedly, he refers to 'the account of the bush' (v 26). The Jews did not possess personal copies of the Old Testament and therefore commonly referred to biblical passages in this general way. Why was this passage so significant? Because it was a part of Scripture which the Sadducees themselves held to be divinely inspired. If it taught the resurrection, the point was proved!

Jesus draws attention to the way in which God speaks of himself as the God of Abraham, Isaac and Jacob. But how does this prove he is the God of the living, not of the dead? Simply because God's covenant promise to save his people would not be of any significance if it were overcome and shattered by death. It would be a tawdry salvation which lasted only for this life. The commitment of God to his servants, Abraham, Isaac, and Jacob, Jesus argued, is itself adequate proof of the resurrection. If the Sadducees had known the power of God as those patriarchs had done, they would realise that hope in God is not for this life only. In a word, Jesus was saying, to deny the resurrection is simply to deny God and his true character. Deny the resurrection and you become a practical atheist.

Know your Bible!

This passage teaches many important lessons. Perhaps the most practical is this: the man who knows the Scriptures and the power of God (as Jesus himself did) will always be able to give an answer for the hope he has in the gospel (1 Pet 3:15). That is why a mind well furnished with Scripture, which has spent time in meditation on its teaching, and is convinced of the power of its author, will see through all hypocritical objections to Christian faith, and be able to contend for the faith which has been given to the church (Jude 3).

56

The Greatest Commandment

Mark 12:28–34

At one point in the Jewish Passover liturgy it seems that a series of questions was asked in preparation for sharing in the sacrament itself. Some careful students of Mark's Gospel have noticed that it too records a series of questions just before the Passover. There is a striking parallel between the Passover liturgy and Mark 12:13–37: the questions involved points of law ('Is it right to pay taxes to Caesar?' Mk 12:14); issues in which the truth was ridiculed (the Sadducees' question about the woman married seven times and the resurrection); questions of conduct (which is the most important commandment?); and finally, a question which the head of the house would put, often seeking the meaning of two passages which seemed contradictory (cf 12:35–7).

If Mark is deliberately following this pattern, then the very way in which he composed the Gospel is meant to say to us: 'Here are the questions which lead up to the true Passover; and here is Jesus, the One who can answer all the questions which the Passover celebrations leave unanswered.' It is a very skilful way of showing the final adequacy of Jesus by contrast with the preliminary nature of all of God's deeds in the Old Testament.

Lawyers and laws

Here, in these verses, a teacher of the law appears who has obviously been listening to the previous debates. He was impressed by what Jesus had to say, and so he too asked a question: 'Which is the most important commandment?'

Questions about which laws are more important than others is a perennial interest of lawyers! This man's question was certainly not original, even though it may have been completely sincere—certainly Jesus treated it as a sincere question, and gave it a straightforward answer.

But, even if the question was sincere, Jesus also seems to indicate that his question was muddle-headed. Quite naturally the lawyer wanted to be able to list the laws of God in a clear order of priority, so that he would know exactly where he stood as he measured his life against them.

Jesus' answer underlined the fact that any man's attempt to measure himself against the law for his own reassurance is bound to lead to disaster, because the very first law requires comprehensive, universal, undiluted love for God with every ounce of one's being. And, it carries with it a clear implication—we are to love our neighbours as ourselves! In other words, Jesus' answer emphasised the fact that God is never satisfied with anything less than the devotion of our whole life for the whole duration of our lives.

Wholehearted devotion

It is important for us to spell out the implications of what Jesus says in his quotation from Deuteronomy 6: 4–5. God is to be the object of the devotion of my heart. The centre of my whole being must be directed towards him and his glory. He must come first in my ambitions and motives. I am to love him too with my soul—so that all my affections and emotions will be in tune with his will and set aflame with a desire to serve him. Then, I must give my thought life to him, seeking to keep my mind pure, and to have all my thinking disciplined and controlled by what he has revealed in Scripture. And all my strength and energy must be his.

My neighbour and myself

But, what does it mean to love our neighbours as ourselves? How can the same Jesus teach us to love self and to deny self (Mk 8:34)?

The answer lies in recognising that God made man as his image. To love God himself implies that we will also love everything which reflects him in any way. It would be inconsistent to love him but not those who bear his image (see James 3:9–10). In this sense, each man should have a proper love and respect for all that God has made him. Notice that loving ourselves is, in the last analysis, the expression of our love for God. That love should be reflected similarly in our attitude to others. We have a special motive for caring for others, as members of the kingdom of God. We know something about people they may not even know about themselves: they were made to reflect God's image and glory. Even what that image has been distorted in their lives, we love them, because we see what they were meant to be, and are moved with compassion.

Here was a law which lifted all law-keeping out of the 'legalism' into which it had sunk in Jesus' day. It was a law which called for total devotion, not merely punctilious observation of a few external rules.

NEAR, BUT NOT IN

The lawyer was clearly impressed by what Jesus said. He recognised that such heartfelt obedience to the Lord was far more important than any ritual in which he could engage without being obedient. Jesus commended him for his understanding, and added a comment designed to send the lawyer home deep in thought: 'You are not far from the kingdom of God' (v 34).

What could that mean? Was this man not actually *in* the kingdom of God, lawyer though he was? Was there a step he still had to take? Indeed there was. He recognised Jesus as a great teacher (v 32). But he was more. He was also the Saviour of those who realised they could not keep the law, and needed not a teacher but a Saviour. This man really was near the kingdom. He recognised great qualities in Jesus. We do not know whether he ever came near enough to Jesus to enter it. What a story he would have to tell if he did!

We are now nearing the end of Mark's record of the coming of the kingdom of God. It is surely time to stop and ask yourself: 'Am I near the kingdom now, or am I actually in it?'

57

Using God's Word

Mark 12:35–44

We have seen Jesus exposed to wave upon wave of attack from his enemies as they acted in unison to try to destroy his ministry. Over and over again, throughout this Gospel, we have noticed the supreme mastery which he displayed. Now, at the end of all the questioning, he shows himself again to be in complete command of the situation. The religious and political leaders could not trap him. Now it was Jesus' turn to ask them a question!

Jesus' question

Jesus believed that the Old Testament was inspired by God. He knew that his destractors shared that view, so he posed this question: 'The scribes say that the Christ is the son of David. How can that be when the Scripture tells us that David himself called the Messiah "Lord"?' Jesus' question depends not only on the scribes believing that the Old Testament was divinely inspired; but also on the fact that they believed Psalm 110 (which Jesus here cites) referred to the promised Messiah. Jesus here was exercising his ministry as the true prophet of God by doing two things.

1. Expounding the scriptures

The scribes were correct to say that the Messiah (Christ) would be the son of David, born in his family line (as, in fact, Jesus was: Matthew 1:1–17; Luke 3:23–32; Romans 1:3). They were also correct in thinking that Psalm 110 described the Messiah. But could they answer the question which arose from those twin convictions? How could the great King David speak of his 'son' as his 'Lord'? No wonder 'the large crowd listened to him with delight' (v 37)! In the battle of difficult questions, Jesus had not only answered questions his opponents regarded as unanswerable; he asked them a question they found unanswerable!!

But our Lord's question was not simply a smart, trick question. It was a deeply serious one. It held a vital clue to the identity of the Messiah. David's son could only be his Lord if he existed before him *and* after him. Jesus did not tell the teachers of the law the answer. It would remain veiled from them so long as they stubbornly resisted Jesus' ministry. But Jesus knew the answer: David's Lord was the eternal Son of God; David's Lord became his 'son' when he was conceived in the womb of Mary and was born in Bethlehem, the city of David. That was the answer to the biblical question which baffled the lawyers.

Notice, however, that in his exposition of the Scriptures, Jesus was doing something else, which all true biblical exposition does:

2. Exposing false teachers

As he continued his teaching (v 38), he warned the people against the teachers who were leading them astray. No doubt there were some among the people who were sufficiently spiritually-minded to feel a deep unease about the influence of the scribes. But perhaps they were too respectful, or too timid to raise their voices. In any case, they doubtless found it almost impossible to put their finger on exactly what made them feel so uneasy. But when Jesus spoke, it all became crystal clear.

Three charges

Jesus brought three specific charges against them—which will, in varying degrees, always be true of false teachers:

1. They were ambitious men

They looked for the honour men can give rather than the honour God alone gives. They were attracted by the trappings of power ('flowing robes' v 38), and the adulation of man ('greeted in the market-places' v 38). Instead of helping those they taught to know, trust and serve God, they used their position to further their own self-centred ambitions and their desire for a reputation.

2. They were proud men

They loved to have the best seats and sit at the table with the 'top' people (v 39) in both secular and religious life. All this was in stark contrast to what one of their number had just heard from the lips of Jesus: love for God and neighbour marked obedience to the law which they professed to teach. Instead they had put love for self at the top of their list, however much they disguised the fact.

3. They were greedy men

They made wealthy widows their prey (v 40), and perhaps poor ones too. These were women whose husbands had, during their lifetime, made all the major decisions for them. Now, lacking that experienced guidance and companionship, they fell prey to these wicked men masquerading as servants of God. Without saying any more, Jesus exposed their despicable lifestyle and their polluted hearts.

PUBLIC MINISTRY ENDED

These solemn words signal the end of Jesus' public ministry in the Gospel of Mark. Throughout the entire period of his ministry, as we have seen, he found himself under constant attack by these religious leaders. He had dealt with them graciously, faithfully, patiently. Now, it seems, they had hardened their hearts irreversibly against him. All that remained for him to do was to unmask their deceit. This he did. His last words to the teachers of the law warned them that they would be 'punished most severely' (v 40).

There is a message here which applies to teachers of God's word today: By their fruits we know whether they are really true to Jesus Christ, or not.

58

A Widow's Mite

Mark 12:41–44

Jesus was a great observer of human experience in general. But he also had an eye for the individual. This wonderful little story illustrates both of these qualities. It describes a woman whose devotion to the Lord stands in marked contrast to that of the educated theologians who had proved to be such a thorn in Jesus' side.

Having finished his teaching in the Temple courts (Mk 12:35), our Lord sat down near the area (in the Court of Women) where visitors to the Temple placed their offerings. It was soon to be Passover. Doubtless Jerusalem was already being flooded with pilgrims from all over the world. Its normal population of 50,000 was increased by some 200,000 pilgrims. Some, like the Ethiopian Eunuch described in Acts 8:27, were certainly people of considerable devotion, influence and wealth. Doubtless some of them were making very substantial contributions indeed.

When you remember two things, this scene is all the more dramatic. On the wall of the Court of Women stood thirteen brass receptacles, in the shape of trumpets. In Jesus' time, of course, there were no banknotes, cheque books or credit cards! Every offering deposited in the receptacles could be 'heard' even if it was not 'seen'! The seats where Jesus sat down and 'watched the crowd putting their money into the temple treasury' (v 41) must have been a popular spot for local people to sit, and perhaps day-dream a little! No doubt there were those around Jesus who were just 'dying to know' what he thought of some of these fabulously rich people and their enormous gifts to God's house!

Two coins in a trumpet

Was there a lull in the excitement after several wealthy pilgrims in succession had put in their gifts, when Jesus saw this poor widow woman come forward to the receptacles? Did nobody else take any real notice of her? Did the crowd—like ourselves sometimes—turn and look elsewhere in case their gaze should embarrass this dear soul who clearly would contribute next to nothing to the Lord's work?

There is something magnificent in Jesus' response here. Did he smile as he heard the almost inaudible tinkle of the widow's two coins fall into the treasury? 'Peter, James, John, Andrew' he called out, 'Over here! Look!' Did he actually go over to the widow, now astonished at the attention she was receiving? We do not know. But we do know what he said: 'This woman has given more than any of the others' (v 43). What a reversal of the disciples' point of view! What a riddle for the crowd to puzzle over! What an unexpected encouragement for the widow, that this should be the divine assessment of her giving!

Not worth twopence?

So emphatic about this is Jesus that he prefaces his remarks with the solemn 'I tell you the truth' (the 'Amen' which appears some thirteen times in Mark's Gospel, and is really equivalent to the Old Testament's 'As I live, says the Lord'). But, how can this be? Surely a thousand pounds is worth far more than one pound, on anybody's arithmetic? Can God not do more with large amounts than with small?

Jesus explains that the divine accountancy works on different principles from the human, and in doing so teaches us several important lessons about Christian giving.

God does not need your money. He requires no benefactors to help him establish his kingdom. Nothing you can do or give will add to his riches. He owns the entire universe, and can employ everything in it for his own holy purposes. Furthermore, he owns your money too! He is able to give it to you and withdraw it from you at a moment's notice. You are simply his steward. Anything you give to him he has first given to you, like a father giving pocket money to his children to help them buy his birthday present!

God chooses to use whatever gifts he wants to further his kingdom. He can use a small gift for a great purpose and a great gift for a small purpose! With a great gift, a massive organisation may be set up which is in constant financial difficulties and eventually goes bankrupt; with a small gift, a Gospel, or New Testament may be purchased which leads to the conversion of someone who wins many others to Christ, or is the instrument of a great revival—or, for that matter, points a millionaire to Christ! Jesus is underlining this in what he says. If we grasped it, we would never be proud of the amount we give.

How to give

But there are three further lessons underlined here:

1. Our giving is to be measured by proportion, not by addition

The woman gave more because she gave everything she had (v 44). Two pence out of two pence is a factor of one; one thousand out of ten thousand is a factor of one tenth!

2. Our giving is not measured by amount, but by sacrifice

This is why Jesus commended the widow. It cost her to give; others might not notice the difference in their bank balances.

3. Our giving is always in the sight of Jesus Christ

It is his estimate that really matters, not the estimate of men.

In most Christian fellowships prayer follows the reception of the offering. That is no formality. For it is not the amount of money given which produces the Lord's blessing on our gifts. We give out of privilege; we need to pray that it will please the Lord to use our gifts as he pleases, and to help us to give in a way that pleases him.

59

Future Events

Mark 13:1–11

Jesus had been teaching in the Temple in Jerusalem. It was the focal point of faith for his contemporaries, as it had been for their forefathers. In a literal sense it was, for them 'the house of God'. He had promised to dwell there, among his people and show them his glory. But in many ways 'Ichabod' (the glory has departed, 1 Samuel 4:21) seemed to be written across it. Externally, it was still able to draw out the deepest emotions of those who worshipped there. It reminded them of earlier days when its courts had rung with praise, and when their forefathers had met with God. It was the symbol of God's restoring of his people from bondage and exile. Yet, when Jesus had come to the Temple of God, he had found it degraded into the centre of commercial enterprise. It had been turned into a 'den of robbers' (Mk 11:17). The only thing Jesus had found in its precincts to commend was the wholehearted devotion of a poor and insignificant widow!

There was no denying that the Temple was impressive. As the disciple band left it, one of them commented on its grandeur (v 1). Immediately Jesus counselled him to see beyond the facade to the reality, and beyond the present to the future: within a generation (see v 30) these buildings would all be destroyed!

The disciples must have been stunned, but they said nothing until they had sat down together on the Mount of Olives, opposite the Temple (v 3). Then three of them raised the question which was on all of their minds. Had they heard him correctly? Had he really prophesied the destruction of God's sacred Temple? For the disciples that could mean only one thing: the end of the world. That is made clear in Matthew's fuller record of the series of questions the disciples asked Jesus: 'When will this happen, and what will be the sign of your coming and of the end of the age?' (Mt 24:3).

Inevitably the disciples associated all these events with one another. When we read through the various accounts in the Gospels of Jesus' teaching, however, we see that he clearly distinguished them from each other.

Significantly, Mark does not even mention the third question about the end of the age. He mentions only the question about the destruction of Jerusalem. In doing so, he helps us to grasp that it is this—the destruction of the Temple and the city—which is the centrepiece of Jesus' discussion in the verses which follow.

Jesus' first word is one of wise counsel, which the church has too often ignored: Do not be deceived (v 5)! What does he mean?

Our Lord knew that many of his followers could easily fall prey to false teachers who would make capital (in more ways than one, alas) out of the distinctively Christian conviction that human history is heading towards a conclusion at the return of Christ. Some people would actually claim to be Christ; others would point to the 'signs of the times'—wars and rumours of wars (v 7), and insist that these events, coupled with natural disasters like earthquakes and famine, are signs that the end of the world is just months away.

Birth pains

It is vital to grasp the significance of Jesus' response to this. These events are simply 'the beginning of birth pains' (v 8). His illustration is apt. Labour pains certainly indicate that a birth is about to take place. But who knows how long a woman's labour may be? The birth pains serve as warnings to be ready, they do not serve as a prophecy of the exact moment of birth. This 'beginning of birth pains' does not tell us whether the end will be tomorrow or next century. Events may be drawn out by God in his patience (2 Pet 3:9) or they may accelerate rapidly. We must always live in readiness and expectation. But we must not allow ourselves to be led into panic by a wrong diagnosis of the 'contractions' in the universe.

To suffer and to witness

Why is this important? Notice Jesus' comments.

1. We may have to endure suffering (v 9a)

There may be persecution to be endured (v 13a). We need to face that realistically. We cannot afford to be blinded to the realities by a false hope (or wish) that the end will come before the Christian life becomes 'too hot to handle' for us.

2. We are to be witnesses to Christ

His purpose is that the gospel must be preached to all people groups (v 10). It is a sad commentary on the church's misunderstanding of this passage that at times Christians have virtually abandoned the task of evangelism because 'the times are evil'. Those are the very times when evangelism is most crucial (see 2 Timothy 3:1–4:5).

Yes, the destruction of the Temple would take place within a matter of decades. It would be an event of such magnitude that the disciples could certainly be forgiven for thinking it would mark the end of everything. But Jesus was teaching them that instead it would mark only the dawning of a new era. Jerusalem could no longer keep the covenant mercy of God within its walls. If it did not recognise the Christ and proclaim him to the nations, its divine purpose would be brought to an end. It would be destroyed. Instead these ordinary men would take the gospel to the four corners of the earth. They would be the dwelling place of God's Spirit; they would be his Temple; they would show forth his glory among the peoples (1 Pet 2:5–9)!

Jesus will come 'soon'. But when Scripture speaks about him coming 'soon', it is measuring time on God's clock, not man's. It means that the return of the Lord is now the next great event on the divine calendar. He has the date marked in red, although no one else has seen either the page of the calendar, or the date he has ringed (see verse 32)! In the meantime, he is working patiently for the salvation of men. Jesus says we should do the same.

60

The Son of Man Comes

Mark 13:12–31

Jesus often used the questions he was asked as opportunities to give instruction to his disciples. He had just prophesied the destruction of the Jerusalem Temple. His disciples associated that with the end of the world. Now he was patiently counselling them not to confuse these two events, lest they be led astray by false teachers. They must recognise the possibility that they might have to face prolonged suffering for the sake of the gospel. In particular, Jesus was concerned to teach the disciples that it was their responsibility to bring the gospel to all peoples. The end would not come before that purpose had been fulfilled (v 10–11).

The interpretation of this section is critical for understanding the whole chapter. For Jesus speaks of 'the end' (v 13) and the 'abomination of desolation' (v 14). He describes events of cosmic magnitude taking place: 'the sun will be darkened and the moon will not give its light' (v 24). He speaks of 'the Son of Man coming in clouds with great power and glory' to gather his elect (vv 26–7). What is he talking about?

THE ABOMINATION OF DESOLATION

At first sight, it might seem obvious that Jesus is speaking here about the second coming. But we ought not to jump to that conclusion without asking what some of these statements (drawn from the language of the Old Testament) would have meant to his hearers. When we do that, it seems more likely that a good deal of what Jesus says here has specific reference to the destruction of Jerusalem, which took place in AD 70.

'The abomination of desolation' was an expression first used by Daniel (Dan 9:27; 11:31; 12:11). It clearly refers to some gross act of sacrilege committed against the Lord. The Jewish people had seen at least one illustration of its meaning when Antiochus Epiphanes had erected an altar to the pagan god Zeus over the altar of burnt offering and, to underline his blasphemy, had sacrificed pigs on it (in 168 BC).

Within the lifetime of some of those who heard Jesus speak, similar actions had been perpetrated within the Temple. Within a few years of Jesus' prophecy, the Roman Emperor Caligula had planned to build a statue of himself on the same altar; then, two years before the Temple was actually destroyed, Jewish zealots perpetrated various atrocities in the Temple, and a clown named Phanni was installed as high priest. The fact that Jesus gives instructions to any disciples in Jerusalem at that time to flee suggests that he is thinking of events within their lifetime. The historian Josephus records that when Titus beseiged Jerusalem in AD 70, somewhere in the region of one million Jews died at that time by crucifixion, famine and other horrors. Our Lord's words were to be literally fulfilled.

Jesus expected his followers to be courageous in their discipleship; but he warned them to avoid the rashness of fanaticism. They were not to think that Jerusalem was so crucial in the purposes of God that they must stay there at all costs. No, more important to them even than the beloved city of Jerusalem was their calling to preach the gospel. They should flee (v 14ff). They should be careful not to be deceived by false 'saviours' who would appear and even work miracles in their sight.

THE SON OF MAN COMES!

It is difficult to know whether verses 24–27 refer to those events in AD 70 or to the end of the age. The language Jesus uses reflects the way in which the Old Testament described the Day of the Lord (Is 13:10; 33:4). But those words may refer to extraordinary political upheavals. And the coming of the Son of Man may refer to his establishing of his kingdom, rather than his coming again. Certainly, in Daniel 7:14 (the source of this idea) the coming of the Son of Man refers to his enthronement at the right hand of God, not to his coming from the right hand of God. In this case, the sending of the 'angels' (literally, 'messengers') would refer to the world-wide proclamation of the gospel which followed the destruction of Jerusalem.

In verses 28–31, Jesus does seem to refer specifically to the destruction of Jerusalem. Just as leaves on the fig tree are normally the sign of the approach of summer, so these events should be a sign to the people (v 29). Notice how he emphasises that these things will happen within the lifetime of that generation (v 30). While this has sometimes been taken to refer to the Jewish people, that is not the most natural interpretation.

Jesus probably never spoke with greater feeling and solemnity. One day even heaven and earth will pass away, he said—but these words would stand for ever!

What are we meant to learn from a passage such as this, which seems to be open to such various interpretations? First, we are urged to listen to what Jesus says, not to what others say. Otherwise we will be easily deceived. We are to be on our guard, since Jesus has spoken to us (v 23).

Secondly, we are not to be taken by surprise by the sufferings of God's people, nor by the catastrophes of history. These are the birthpangs which herald the dawning of a new age. Thirdly, we require a good dose of common sense in living the Christian life—Jesus warns his disciples not to invite suffering unnecessarily (vv 14–20). Yes, God will guard his people; but he guards them through their obedience to Jesus' commands.

We see here, again, that when Jesus speaks about the future, his words are meant to change the way we live in the present. That is a recurring theme in all Biblical teaching about the time to come.

61

Be Prepared

Mark 13:32–37

In reading the New Testament, one of the features we should always look out for is the connection between the truth and its practical application. Often that application is very clearly spelled out, since it flows inevitably from the teaching of the gospel. We find exactly the same here. Jesus has been teaching his disciples about the destruction of the Temple, and distinguishing that event from the great event of his personal return. But one thing binds both events together: the response the disciples are to make in their lives.

This is characteristic of the apostles' teaching about the future: in the light of what is going to happen, we are to live lives which bring honour to Christ. We are to respond appropriately to God's activity in human history. In this closing section of Mark 13, Jesus spells out what this implies.

Jesus tells a parable about a man who goes away from home leaving his servants in charge. They are to live in the consciousness that the master may return at any time. They are to look after his affairs faithfully in the meantime.

THE MASTER'S HOUSE

What does Jesus mean? He reminds us that the 'house' in which we have been left in charge is not ours, but his. How often we act as though we had forgotten this! Frequently, when there is division among the people of God, it is because this 'family rule' has been forgotten. We act as though we owned the church, and as if what we found acceptable was the principle on which it should be structured. We need to remember that we live in the master's house, not our own. We have a responsibility to him.

APPOINTED TASKS

But Jesus also stresses that each individual in his household has an appointed task (v 24). There is, for example 'one at the door' (v 34); others have different roles to play. But all of the servants in a well-ordered household know what their role is, and attend to it. Only when each individual fulfils his or her own task does the household run smoothly (cf Eph 4:11–16). There is an element of responsibility; there is also an element of individuality.

All of the servants are to share one attitude to their work and ministry: they are to labour in the consciousness that the owner of the house will return. The date is unknown (v 32). We should therefore be alert, keeping awake, doing our duty, as we wait for him to return (vv 33–6).

WAITING FOR THE RETURNING LORD

This is one of the cardinal principles of true Christian living: to live every day in the light of Christ's certain return; to do everything—yes, everything—for his inspection. Christians do not necessarily have better skills than others who make no Christian profession; but they do have the strongest of motives to use their skills properly, in readiness for their Heavenly Master's comments. That is why everything we do should in some way reflect the grace and glory of Christ and be part of our witness to him.

The early Christians did not always understand Jesus' teaching. In Thessalonica, for example, some members of the church seem to have abandoned their daily work because they believed that Christ would return soon (2 Thess 3:6–15). In the light of that event (so they mistakenly thought) work was far too unspiritual. But the true fruit of expectancy in the life of a Christian is the quality of his daily work and the glory which surrounds his fulfilment of his daily duty. That is what our Lord expects us to be doing when he returns.

Faithfulness

How would you spend tomorrow if you knew Jesus was going to return in the evening? John Wesley was once asked that question as he made his way from one preaching engagement to another. He took out his diary, read the list of engagements he had for the following day, and said 'And that is what I would do tomorrow if I knew the Lord was returning then.' That is the way Jesus challenges all of us to live.

How sad it is that instead of seeing this teaching about the future as the spur to new obedience and faithfulness, it has often been the excuse for either controversy or laziness in the Christian church. That has been true from the days of the first churches until now (as the New Testament letters show). We must remember to read such passages as Mark 13 with great humility of mind. But we must also remember that they summon us to rigorous, practical obedience to the Lord. If what we have learned in this chapter does not make us more watchful as Christians, then we have not yet allowed Jesus to have the last word in our lives. For his last word here is precisely that: 'What I say to you, I say to everyone: "Watch"' (v 37).

Since you do not know when your Master will return (vv 32, 33, 35), are you awake, and watching?

62

Love for Jesus

Mark 14:1–11

When you read Mark 13 with its vivid record of Jesus' teaching, it is not difficult to imagine yourself on the Mount of Olives, looking across to the Temple—transported for a moment beyond the present world into the great vision of the future which Jesus portrayed. But now Mark brings us back from the future into the harsh realities which faced Jesus in the present.

When Jesus was in the Temple, among his enemies, his one source of encouragement lay in the wholehearted sacrificial lifestyle of a widow woman who had put all she had into the offering. That must have been a remarkable thing for Mark's first readers to discover in such a male-orientated society. It is not insignificant that, in this scene, set apparently among Jesus' friends, it is once again the action of a woman which stands out as a source of blessing to our Lord.

We are now entering the closing section of the Gospel. From now on, Mark's record describes the events which lead up to the cross with the careful precision of a diarist. He notes the day (and sometimes even the time of day) of one event after another. Here he begins by telling us that as the Passover drew near, the religious leaders were committed to arresting and killing Jesus. They wanted to find some 'sly way' (v 1) to do it. They also wanted to avoid killing him during the feast, in case riots broke out in the overcrowded city. By verse 11, their 'prayers' have been answered in the way they least expected: Judas, the treasurer of the disciple band had agreed to betray his Master!

A WOMAN'S ACTION

Just at this point, Mark introduces a story which seems like a 'pause' in the narrative, but in fact partly explains what follows. He describes an event which stands (again) in marked contrast to the conniving hatred of the religious leaders.

Jesus was in Bethany, some two miles from Jerusalem, dining with a man known as Simon the Leper (perhaps because Jesus had cured him). A woman broke open a jar of expensive ointment and poured its contents over Jesus' head, in an act of anointing.

Three elements in what followed are important:

1. Action

This lady brought with her a jar of perfume which the disciples valued at more than an average man's wages for an entire year. Presumably this was a family heirloom, passed on from generation to generation; it was an investment for a 'rainy day' in this woman's life. But, at this moment in this woman's spiritual pilgrimage she had a reason to be grateful to Jesus. In a moment of quiet commitment she had resolved that he should receive her most precious possession. Quietly she had taken it from its place, and carried it to Simon's house, where Jesus was. In gratitude for the past, she poured her 'future' and her 'security' on Jesus. No wonder he described her action as 'beautiful'!

2. Reaction

Some of the spectators were indignant (v 4). They knew that if the perfume had been sold and the proceeds given to the poor, it could have done so much good. And so they harshly rebuked the woman (v 5).

The harshness of their response underlines the remaining hardness in their hearts, and perhaps also the poverty of their own devotion to the Lord. It is significant that this particular event seemed to act as the catalyst to bring Judas and the chief priests together (vv 10–11). The one thing he could not tolerate, apparently, was such wholehearted devotion to Jesus which had no other motive than love for him. Judas was one of those religious people who rarely see that their interest in Christ lies more in what he can do to further their goals than in what he wants to do to change their lives. He, with others, could not tell the difference between grace and waste. Their attitude indicated that they understood all too little of the outpouring of grace in Jesus' heart towards sinners!

3. Commendation

Jesus responded to the woman with joyful appreciation. Yes, the money could have been given to the poor. But it had been given to the poor—to Jesus himself, who for our sake had become poor so that we might become rich (2 Cor 8:9). Unlike the others, this woman had some inkling that Jesus would not be with them much longer, while the 'other' poor would always be present. In this sense, she had anointed Jesus for his burial. 'She did what she could' (v 8). Her critics had done nothing. For that reason her deed is a perpetual memorial of the true response to the one who became poor that we might become rich.

The presence of a grudging spirit towards Christ and his work in the world is always a sinister sign. Here were men who were more interested in their service than in their Master! How sad that so many of Jesus' disciples seem to live so much of their lives grudgingly. The lesson Jesus pointed out to his disciples from this woman was: in the Christian life there should be neither holding back nor turning back.

Are those lessons we have learned?

63

The Traitor

Mark 14:12–21

It was now the time of the Passover. As thousands of pilgrims crowded into Jerusalem for the feast, the disciples' minds turned to the obvious question: what were they going to do about the Passover meal? Where should they go to make preparations (v 12)?

There was force in such a question. Where could they go if Jesus was to be secure? There was a price on his head, as John's Gospel indicates: 'the chief priests and Pharisees had given orders that if anyone found out where Jesus was, he should report it so that they might arrest him' (Jn 11:57). We also know, now, that Judas had agreed to betray him. His life was in grave danger.

Secrecy without fear

The first thing to notice, in this connection, is the secrecy of Jesus' arrangements. Two of the disciples are told to go into the city. There they will see a man carrying a water jar on his head. That was an unusual sight. Normally only the women carried these jars; men carried wineskins. Presumably this was a prearranged signal. This man would be their 'contact' who would lead them to the room where they could prepare for the Passover.

Jesus did not make such arrangements out of fear. When we read the 'Upper Room Discourse' in John 14–17, or listen in this Gospel to the institution of the Lord's Supper, we realise how burdened he must have been to have a few hours of complete privacy with his followers. He wanted to lead them further in their knowledge of God's purposes. His secrecy was the part of wisdom, not fear. The fact that he knew he was to die did not mean that he should simply abandon himself to his foes. That in itself is an important lesson for us to learn.

Surely not I?

In this context, a further revelation takes place. Jesus tells the disciples that the betrayal he had prophesied earlier (Mk 10:33) would arise within their own group. His earlier use of the word 'betray' had hinted at this. But doubtless none of them had really taken in what that implied. Even now they could not believe it. One by one they asked, 'Is it I?'

Judas too, apparently, used these words. Perhaps that was the reason Jesus spoke so sternly about the terrible responsibility he would bear. It would have been better that he had never been born (v 21). Judas' later suicide indicates that he realised this—too late. His eyes were opened to the terrible crime he had committed, and he died in utter despair. But, as Jesus' last pleadings and warnings were issued, Judas was both blind and deaf to his overtures. Even though our Lord warned him of the terrible consequences of his sin, his heart seems to have remained unmoved.

Sin's dominion

Judas is the example *par excellence* of the man who believes that he can never sin his way out of the grace of God. We should remember him if we ever think we can decide the point at which we will stop sinning. Sin deceives as well as hardens. It leads us to that hardness of heart and blindness of understanding which ignores the last amber light. Ultimately even the warnings of the Son of God through his word are silenced. If we yield to sin (as Judas had done in his heart, for whatever reason) it masters us (Jn 8:34). We are no longer free or able to choose the moment when we will engage in a mutiny of grace and overthrow its influence on us. Judas realised that when it was too late. At first he would not repent; eventually he could not repent.

Scripture fulfilled

But these important considerations should not make us ignore the remarkable poise and dignity which Jesus himself shows in the midst of this great crisis in his life. He knows that all of these things will take place 'just as it had been written' (v 21). His life is completely submitted to his Father's will. That will has been revealed in Scripture, and he bows to it. Because his life is governed by the teaching of Scripture, his death will be neither accident nor tragedy.

At no point in Jesus' ministry is his submission to Scripture more frequently mentioned than in these last hours of his life. This is one of the clearest indications that he recognised it to be God's living word. That, in turn, is one of the most important reasons why Christians should believe Scripture. But, notice, Jesus did not believe Scripture in a merely hypothetical or theoretical way. He believed it and obeyed it without compromise. In this, too, he is the 'pioneer of our salvation'. When he calls us to obey God's word, he summons us to follow him, not to go over uncharted ground. He has gone before, and proved that God's word can be relied on in the darkest hours of life and death.

Of course, our lives do not fulfil prophecy as Jesus did. Yet the same Spirit who inspired Scripture, and strengthened Jesus to understand and obey it, has been given to us. The sign that I truly follow Christ and am filled with his Spirit will therefore be this: submission to God's Word!

64

The Last Supper

Mark 14:22–26

The preparation had all been made for Jesus and his disciples to share the Passover together. They were reclining at table, in the middle of the meal. It was an event to which Jesus had looked forward with special eagerness (Lk 22:15)—eagerness to do what he had to do, and, doubtless, eagerness that the darkest hours of his life should be faced in obedience to his Father. Now, after years of patient preparation, the time had come. No more waiting would be required, only the endurance of the terrible agony of the Cross, and his separation from fellowship with God and man. Yet, even this he would endure, encouraged by 'the joy that was set before him' (Heb 12:2).

The Passover

The Passover meal was a beautiful and moving ritual. It was conducted by the head of the house (in this instance, Jesus himself as the leader of the disciple band). Several cups of wine were drunk during the course of the evening. The first was brought in and drunk before the arrival of the traditional Passover food (unleavened bread, bitter herbs, stewed fruit, greens and roast lamb). When the food was brought in, the youngest person would ask the traditional question: 'Why do we eat these foods on this night?'

In reply the father would recount the story of God's grace in the Exodus. The company would respond with songs of praise and sing Psalms 113–115. Then the second cup would be passed round. Just before the meal itself was eaten, the plate of unleavened bread was lifted up, with the words 'This is the bread of affliction which our fathers ate in the land of Egypt. Let everyone who hungers come and eat; let everyone who is needy come and eat the Passover meal'. The father would give thanks for the bread, and break off a piece for each person present. It would then be passed round from one to another.

New bread and wine

The bread was normally eaten in the silence which followed. But on this occasion Jesus spoke: 'I myself am the Passover Bread'. His life would be given as a substitute for his people!

The meal then began, and when it was completed, the father took the third cup of wine, blessed it and passed it round. Psalms 116–118 were then sung and the Passover celebration concluded with the drinking of a fourth cup.

It was as the third cup of wine was about to be drunk that Jesus interjected a further 'new' note into the celebration. This cup was the cup of the new covenant sealed in his blood! Just as blood had been shed in the Passover, his blood would be shed 'for many'. They were to drink from this cup as an expression of their communion with him, and their share in all that he would do for them in forging that covenant with God.

The final 'difference' in this Passover celebration now followed. Jesus announced that they would not drink the fourth cup: 'I will not drink again of the fruit of the vine' (v 25). But, rather than abbreviating their fellowship, he was indicating to them that he planned to extend it, and so he added 'until that day when I drink it anew in the kingdom of God'. The cup which usually brought the Passover to an end would now be drunk at the beginning of the time of endless fellowship in God's kingdom!

With these words ringing in their ears, and Christ's teaching vividly and visually presented to them, they sang the traditional closing praises from Psalms 116–118, and made their way to the Mount of Olives (v 26). In this simple way, Jesus inaugurated the Lord's Supper.

The Lord's Supper

This Christian sacrament has been a focal point for some of the most painful disagreements in the history of Christianity. Is there any way we can relearn what Jesus was teaching his disciples so that when we share in the Lord's Supper together we can 'follow his example in word and in deed'?

There are four key elements in Mark's account of the Last Supper.

1. It celebrates the 'new covenant' which God makes with us through Christ

He is the passover lamb, sacrificed for us (1 Cor 5:7). His death accomplishes the new exodus (cf Lk 9:31, where, as we have already noticed, the Greek word 'exodus' is used to describe what Jesus accomplished on the cross).

What is so important about this? Jesus' sacrifice is the means by which God binds sinners to himself and brings them deliverance from bondage in sin.

2. It focuses our attention on Jesus himself

He inaugurated the Lord's Supper while he was still with them so that they would not be confused about what he meant when he said 'this is my body, this is my blood' (vv 22, 24). The fact that he was present with them made it unmistakably clear that these elements were symbols of Jesus himself—they were not magically transformed into something else. That is a vital lesson to learn: in the Lord's Supper our attention is not focused on the bread and the wine, but on the Lord Jesus who gives them to us.

3. It underlines the importance of communion with Jesus

The sharing of the bread and the wine was a sign of sharing in the blessings of the Passover; the eating and drinking of the 'new' bread and wine is a symbol of our fellowship with Jesus in all he has done for us. Taking the bread and drinking the wine symbolises taking him as Saviour and Lord!

4. It reminds us of the incompleteness of the Christian life

The Last Supper was an unfinished meal; the last cup remained on the table, untouched. In the same way, the Communion service in our churches is an 'unfinished meal'. We are proclaiming the Lord's death 'until he comes' (1 Cor 11:26). Like the first disciples, we should rise from the table eagerly looking forward to the day when we will drink with Jesus in his Father's kingdom!

65

Jesus' Clear Sightedness

Mark 14:27–31

One of the outstanding features of Mark's Gospel is the poise and authority of Jesus. Now that we are in the closing scenes of his life, that becomes all the clearer: Jesus, who is the victim, the One who is about to enter the darkness of Gethsemane and the deep darkness of Calvary, is the only one who is really in control of himself and the situation. In this short section, Mark indicates several things about Jesus which help us to understand the reasons for his dignity. In essence that may be summed up like this: Jesus saw in his situation what no one else had eyes to see.

Scripture fulfilled

Jesus saw that Scripture was being fulfilled. He knew that his friends would abandon him as they were overcome with fear, for Scripture foretold that when God's Shepherd was smitten, the sheep would be scattered (Zech 13:7, quoted here in v 27). He knew himself to be the Shepherd of whom the prophet had spoken. He knew that the smiting was his death, foretold by Isaiah 53:4. It was because this teaching of Scripture had saturated his heart and mind that nothing could ultimately surprise him and unbalance him.

This was true in a unique sense of Jesus. But Peter recognised that in his suffering Jesus was also giving his disciples 'an example that you should follow in his steps' (1 Pet 2:21). The word he uses for 'example' would have been used of a teacher showing a child to write by writing a letter and asking the child to copy it below. This is exactly what Jesus does. 'Look how my life was marked by a poise which came from my submission to my Father's word. Now, you copy that.'

The hand of God

Jesus also saw the hand of God in his experience. One of the reasons for the disciples' failure was that they saw only the terrible circumstances they were in. Their vision was filled with the sight of opposition and danger. Jesus saw that too. But he could see beyond it, to the hand of God. That was why he placed special emphasis on the identity of the One who would smite and bruise him. It would be 'I'—The Great I Am of the Old Testament—God his Father! However painful that thought was to him, he also recognised that he could trust his Father implicitly. Not one blow would fall upon him that was unnecessary for the salvation of men. It was because of this implicit trust that Jesus endured so faithfully.

Failure among disciples

Jesus saw into his disciples' hearts and knew that they would fail. 'You will all fall away' he said (v 27). That included Peter, despite his protests to the contrary. That is why, although he must have been deeply pained by his disciples' failures, he was not really taken by surprise. He was safeguarded from a disappointment which leads to bitterness because he saw the real state of human nature.

The marvel is that Jesus did not love Peter any less. Even although he would deny him three times, Jesus loved him. Later, when Jesus' three-fold questioning by the morning fire on the shore of Galilee must have reminded him of his denial, Peter at last confessed. 'Lord, you know all things...you know that for all my failures, I really do love you' (Jn 21:15–17).

This is something we need to remember about Jesus when we fail. Our sins can easily harden our hearts against him and blind us to his grace. Do not think that he is ever taken by surprise when you fail him. Go to him immediately, and confess your sin, and the weakness of your love for him. He has not been taken by surprise.

Future joy

Jesus saw the resurrection which lay ahead of him. Notice what he says in verse 28 (words which the disciples were too preoccupied to take in until later—Mark 16:7): 'After I have risen...'. He knew that he would triumph over darkness and death and rise again. That did not lessen the heaviness of Gethsemane or the darkness of Calvary. But it did enable him to 'endure the cross and despise the shame', because he could see beyond it to 'the joy that was set before him' (Heb 12:2).

Principles for living

Here, then, are four principles by which every Christian should live.

1. Submit the whole of your life to Scripture

It is the rock on which all spiritual stability will be built.

2. Focus on what God is doing in your circumstances

Do not worry about what man or nature are doing. You may not at first recognise his footprints, but believe that they are there, and be assured that he is working out his perfect purpose in the midst of the chaos around you.

3. Trust your fellow Christians

However, do not forget that we are saints, not angels. We ourselves fail; others fail us; Christ alone is unfailing. Put your trust first in him, and learn to live within the fellowship of failures knowing that he will never fail you.

4. Remember that all the enigmas of life will never be resolved until the resurrection

When the darkness of your present experience seems to make God's hand utterly invisible, look beyond the darkness to the dawning of that morning when the shadows will flee away and 'God will wipe away every tear' from your eyes (Rev 7:17).

66

The Sacred Heart of Christ

Mark 14:32–41

The Garden of Gethsemane is one of the most sacred and solemn scenes in the entire Bible. Such was the intensity of Jesus' experience there that Luke, the physician, recorded that Jesus' sweat was like globules of blood. At the end of the experience, 'an angel from heaven appeared to him and strengthened him' (Lk 22:43). Alexander Whyte, a famous Scottish minister in the nineteenth century once said, with insight, that in heaven, after he had seen Christ himself, he would like his first conversation to be with this angel. Who knows what depths of suffering this angel came to witness?

Mark's account includes three special elements in Jesus' agony in the Garden.

Jesus' feelings

The first element is that of our Lord's mental condition. Only rarely in the Gospels are we told about Jesus' inner attitude to his experiences. But here we learn that he was 'deeply distressed and troubled' (v 33). The language used here is very strong indeed; it conveys the idea of a man who is far away from home and feels abandoned, longing for companionship but finding none. It is clear that Jesus' whole being was profoundly shaken as he began to feel the weight of his coming suffering. Nor did he hide this from his dearest friends: 'My soul is overwhelmed with sorrow to the point of death' he told them (v 34).

Jesus was about to be exposed to the one thing in life he really feared: not the cruel death which would end it (he knew he would rise again), but the indescribable experience of feeling himself to be God-forsaken. He felt he could not live—indeed, that life was not worth living—without the consciousness of his Father's love for him.

Yet the fact that he entered that darkness and experienced such grief is the source of all our comfort. It assures us that he understands our darkest hours. But more, it means that he has drawn the sting from our darkest hour; for he has entered our God-forsaken condition, that we might share his God-accepted relationship to the Father!

Jesus' Submission

The second element in this story focusses on Jesus' submission to the Father.

He prayed that the cup the Father was giving him might be taken away. (This, incidentally, teaches us that it is not necessarily wrong to ask for something which God does not intend to do, so long as our hearts are prepared to submit to his will, whatever that is.) This 'cup' was something he had spoken about before (see Mark 10:38). It had been employed by the Old Testament prophets as a symbol of the outpoured judgement of God (Is 51:17, 22; Jer 25:15, 17; Ezek 23:31–3; Hab 2:16). Drinking it meant shame before men and alienation from God. Jesus knew that, and in his perfect humanity shrank from it. Had he not done so, we could never have believed him to be fully, as well as truly human. Yet his Father's will was that he should drink it, and to that will he submitted.

Everything in Jesus longed to escape from this terrible experience, seen in its own light; yet everything in Jesus also longed to be obedient to the Father—and in that light he bowed before him, praying 'Not my will, but your will, be done, Father'. So he took the cup. Never in the Gospels does the humanity of Jesus shine through more clearly; never in the Gospels does his holiness appear more forcibly.

JESUS' DISAPPOINTMENT

The third element in Jesus' consciousness here is his tremendous sense of disappointment in his disciples. He had already prophesied that they would desert him (v 27). But it would be a mistake to conclude from this that Jesus did not feel their failure keenly. He had asked them to watch and pray. He needed them as guards at his final time of prayer in the garden. He urged them to pray with him lest they find themselves exposed and powerless in the testing time which was about to come. But they failed him miserably. Time and again they heard him urge them to watch and pray; time and again they could not summon the resources to stay awake with their Master. In the light of that it is no surprise to read later in the chapter that 'everyone deserted him and fled' (v 50).

Jesus remained faithful when his heart was breaking, when the cup was bitter and when his companions were weak. In the light of this Peter's words are all the more challenging—when we remember that he was there, with Jesus in Gethsemane: 'Christ suffered for you, leaving an example, that you should follow in his steps' (1 Pet 2:21).

The implication is clear. Without his faithfulness in Gethsemane, he would not have been faithful 'unto death' on Calvary. This test was a prelude and preparation for that test. It is always the case. We need to learn to 'watch and pray' in our current situation, or we will never be able to do so when the 'evil day' comes.

Gethsemane was unique. We do not go through our own Gethsemane. Jesus has done that for us. But we must learn to place our feet in the footsteps of faithfulness which he planted there, if we are to be his disciples.

67

Left Alone

Mark 14:43–52

This fourteenth chapter in Mark's Gospel began with an intimation of what was taking place 'behind the scenes' as Jesus and his disciples were together in the Upper Room sharing in the Passover meal, and then in the Garden of Gethsemane. The religious leaders were plotting to kill Jesus. Now their plot had been activated.

Judas Iscariot had been present in the Upper Room, but had left during the evening (see John 13:30). Having already arranged to betray Jesus (Mk 14:10–11), he now went to make the last-minute arrangements. He knew that Jesus would go to the Garden of Gethsemane, and so he led an armed crowd there to capture him. In the narrative describing what followed, several things stand out for comment.

Intimidated by Jesus?

The fear in the hearts of Jesus' enemies stands out. They came to arrest him 'armed to the teeth' (v 43). Jesus immediately pointed out how sinister this was (v 48). He was no revolutionary! Words of violence had never crossed his lips. He had never used any of his gifts for destructive purposes—yet religious leaders were sending this gang of armed men to hound him down!

Inherent in Jesus' words is a moral appeal to those who had come with Judas. Our Lord knew they did not bear the ultimate guilt. They were acting thoughtlessly, under instruction from their seniors. He knew that they would carry out their orders. But he wanted to speak to their consciences in a way that might be used later to convict them of their own sin and of his own righteousness. For all we know some of them may have been convicted when Peter preached on the Day of Pentecost (see Acts 2:36ff).

It is clear that our Lord's enemies were intimidated by him, and by the holiness of his life. Those who are religious but antagonistic to Christ always are intimidated by him, and seek to silence him by force and by numbers. This should have been a solemn warning to the Christian church throughout the ages. How tragic that sometimes those who have had authority in the church have sought to silence the voice of Christ by force!

The traitor

The second sad feature of this narrative is the dishonesty of Judas the traitor. He gave the prearranged signal—the one he kissed was the one who should be arrested. With a sign of devotion he betrayed the Lord (vv 44–5).

The fact that a sign was even needed underlines the fact that those who came to arrest Jesus came by night. In the dim light, only someone who knew Jesus well would have been able to distinguish him from the others. If the arrest was legitimate, they should have made it during the day—as Jesus indicates (v 49). Was this an appeal to Judas? Or was his conscience so seared now that he could not see the illegal actions in which he had involved himself? Months before this event took place, when Judas was the well-respected treasurer of the disciple band, he would probably have been incapable of believing that any of the disciples could do such a thing. But he had begun to steal from the disciples' fund. He had taken what belonged to his fellows. He had taken what belonged to Jesus! Was it the case with Judas, as with others, that he was driven to hide those 'small' sins, until he would choose to have Jesus murdered rather than himself discovered? At the end of the day, betraying Christ came more easily to him than confessing his sin. His tragedy has often been repeated. He stands as a warning to us when we fall into sin: openly confess it to Christ, and be cleansed, or the darkness in your heart may one day engulf your whole soul.

Panic

Mark also records the panic of the disciples (v 50). Their failure was clearly not of the same magnitude as Judas's. It displayed their weakness rather than their callousness. But it was not the weakness of a moment, as we have seen. It was the result of failing to build a solid foundation in watching and praying earlier in the evening. They had been more conscious of their tiredness than of their frailty. They were not the last of whom that was true. Like Judas, they stand before us as memorials of what can take place when we give in to weakness which we regard as 'justifiable' until we taste its consequences.

Serenity

Finally, we should notice once again the serenity of Jesus in the midst of this injustice. He is in complete control. It is he who explains the underlying significance of what is taking place. It is because 'the Scriptures must be fulfilled' (v 50). The Man who knows that God will always keep his word is the One whose 'ordered life' confesses the 'beauty of God's peace'.

A STRANGE FOOTNOTE

Mark's record of the arrest concludes with what at first sight is a strange footnote. A young man was following Jesus. He was seized, and in his panic to escape, fled naked, leaving his linen garment behind. Such garments were expensive, indicating that this young man came from a wealthy family—as Mark himself seems to have done. Perhaps it was Mark himself. Whether it was or not, the event is reminiscent of Amos' description of the day of God's judgement when even the bravest of men would 'flee naked on that day' (Amos 2:16). What to other observers was the beginning of the trial and last judgement of Jesus was, also, the trial and last judgement of the Jewish leaders. Jesus was being left entirely alone. In what he was about to do no one would stand with him. No one could. He would stand alone as Saviour because he alone was fit to bear the judgement of God in our place.

68

Witnessing a Good Confession

Mark 14:53–65

Jesus was now brought before the Sanhedrin (v 53). It was the highest ruling court of the Jews, and was modelled on Moses and his seventy elders. It had the strictest rules to guard against any miscarriage of justice. It also had wide powers, although during the Roman occupation of Palestine it could not normally carry out a death sentence. This is the reason why, after his condemnation by the religious court, Jesus was taken to the Roman procurator Pontius Pilate and accused of treason which was a capital offence in Roman law.

Despite its constitution, however, it is clear that a basic miscarriage of true justice took place in the case of Jesus. Mark records that—however they might follow the constitutional procedures outwardly—the Sanhedrin members were deliberately looking for a way of removing Jesus from the scene (v 55). The court was far from impartial. In normal circumstances the rules of the Sanhedrin gave the benefit of the doubt to the accused. But it is clear that some of its members had already decided on a verdict of 'guilty' for Jesus even before the trial had begun. They wanted to put him to death (v 55). So they brought false witnesses forward. But their testimony did not agree (a point of great importance in Jewish law, which should have stood in Jesus' favour, but simply incited his opponents all the more).

The True Witness

In contrast to these false witnesses, our Lord stood before the Sanhedrin as the 'faithful and true witness' (Rev 1:5). When false charges were brought against him, he said nothing. Symbolically he emphasised that no genuine charge had been brought against him. There was no substantiated accusation to answer. He did not need to respond. No doubt Jesus was remembering (and was reminding those members of the court who still had some spiritual sensitivity) Isaiah's prophecy about the Servant of the Lord: 'He was oppressed and afflicted, yet he did not open his mouth...as a sheep before her shearers is silent, so he did not open his mouth' (Is 53:7). Did some of them 'hear' what Jesus was saying without opening his mouth?

But later Jesus did speak, when the high priest questioned him directly (and under oath, Matthew 26:63): 'Are you the Christ, the Son of the Blessed One?'

I am the Messiah

Jesus now revealed the identity which he had kept veiled throughout his ministry. Yes, he was the Messiah—although not the kind expected by the Jews, as they all knew well. Indeed, he went further. He was combining several Old Testament figures to express his identity: he stood before them as the Suffering Servant; he had confessed to being the Messiah; now he revealed himself as the Son of Man, described in Daniel 7:13–14.

In his vision Daniel saw

> one like a son of man, coming with the clouds of heaven.

> He approached the Ancient of Days and was led into his presence. He was given authority, glory and sovereign power; all peoples, nations and men of every language worshipped him. His dominion is an everlasting dominion that will not pass away, and his kingdom is one that will never be destroyed.

Jesus, whom the Sanhedrin proposed to judge, was claiming to be the king and judge of all the earth!

No examination of this claim needed to be made—at least in the opinion of the Sanhedrin. How could this man, deserted by his followers, standing powerless before them, possibly be the glorious Messiah of the Jewish people? The idea was—to the high priest anyway—blasphemous. He tore his robes and called for a verdict of guilty. Jesus was condemned as worthy of death (v 64).

Undiluted hatred

The final verse of this passage tells us what religious men may become when they have rejected Jesus Christ: beasts of passion. They sought to belittle Jesus by spitting on him; they mocked him by blindfolding him, striking him and calling on him to show he was the Messiah by 'prophesying' who had hit him. Who would believe these gentleman scholars could be so vitriolic? How could they spit on the Son of God and then hand him over to their law officers for more of the same treatment?

The scene would be incredible were it not for the fact that it has been repeated down through history. Many a follower of Christ has been treated in this way, simply because of faithfulness to the Lord. As with Jesus, so with his disciples: the light reveals much that has been hidden in the darkness.

Later in his ministry, Simon Peter wrote of Jesus as our example in suffering. He had this scene in mind (which perhaps he heard even if he did not see: verses 53–

4, 66). 'When they hurled their insults at him he did not retaliate; when he suffered he made no threats. Instead he 'entrusted himself to him who judges justly' (1 Pet 2: 22–23).

> In my place, condemned, he stood
> Sealed my pardon with his blood
> Hallelujah! What a Saviour!

69

The Crumbling Rock

Mark 14:66–72

Poor Peter! He loved his Master too much to desert him absolutely, and so he had followed him 'at a distance' (v 54), and at considerable personal risk. Yet he loved himself too much to be able to remain indifferent to the consequences of all-out faithfulness. It is instructive to realise that he is better remembered for his denial than he is for the degree of faithfulness he demonstrated. Sometimes we malign Peter. We should remember that he was the only one of the disciples who took even this risk. But his testimony underlines the fact that even the bravest and brashest of them failed on that night.

Peter Tested

Mark here records the progress of Peter's testing. First, the servant girl thinks she has seen Peter somewhere before. Perhaps she had seen the disciple band when they had been together in the Temple earlier in that week. In the flickering night lights she needed to peer through the gloom to be absolutely sure (v 67). Yes, it was the same man—and she said so!

Peter denied the girl's statements in the most general

of terms. He did a 'typical cover-up'. But his actions spoke for themselves. With a guilty conscience he went out into the entry way, perhaps hoping that distanced from the light he could remain unrecognised. But the servant girl was not to be outdone. Passing by the entry she spoke again, only this time she appealed to those around her. 'You are one of them' she insisted (v 70). But again Peter denied it.

As the moments passed, perhaps Peter gradually made his way back into the courtyard proper. He was certainly anxious for his Master. Did he fall into conversation with those around him? Now his accent betrayed him. So they pressed him: 'You are a Galilean! You must be one of his disciples' (v 70). The flood-gates of self control were broken open; in the most solemn terms Peter denied his Lord. Calling down curses on himself if he were telling a lie, he insisted he did not know Jesus!

At that moment, three things happened, almost simultaneously: a rooster crowed; the sound was mingled in Peter's mind with something else—Jesus' voice saying 'Before the rooster crows twice, you will disown me three times' (v 72). You can almost hear Peter telling this story in his preaching, and adding, 'I broke down and wept' (v 72).

Weakness yields easily

This moving part of the Gospel of Mark is intended to teach us some important lessons. One of them is that our personal weaknesses need only the least pressure from temptation to bring us to our knees. There was something admirable about the way Peter had followed Jesus. But there was also something tragic about it: he still did not take seriously his Master's searching analysis of his moral failures. The enquiries of a servant girl were enough to draw out from him the horrible realities of his own heart. He put himself first, before his Lord. He would disown his Lord rather than deny himself.

Jesus' eyes

Peter was without excuse, and in the mercy of Christ he realised it. We know from Luke 22:61 that at the very moment of his denial, he looked across the courtyard and met the eyes of Jesus. That was to be his salvation, for he saw in those eyes not condemnation but compassion. That was the turning point in his life. Jesus had tried to 'break him down' many times before. Now, in this most painful and memorable of ways, Peter saw himself as he really was, repented, and was remade into the great apostle.

Judas and Peter

In the closing section of the Gospel, Peter and Judas are placed side by side. Both fail. But while one was lost, the other was saved. Where did the difference lie?

We can answer that question on several levels. We could delve into the mystery of God's sovereign working in men's lives, and try to answer it. But Scripture tends to answer it on a different level altogether: Peter remembered the Lord's word, wept bitterly, and turned to Jesus for forgiveness. He placed his hope in the promise of restoration Christ had given to him ('When you are restored, strengthen your brothers' Lk 22:31–2).

By stark contrast, Judas had no hope, only regret. Both men knew despair; but Judas despaired of God and of grace; Peter despaired of self, and found hope in Christ and his word.

Of all men, perhaps, Peter is the clearest New Testament example of the experience of Psalm 130: 'If you, O Lord, kept a record of sins, O Lord, who could stand?

But with you there is forgiveness; therefore you are feared. I wait for the Lord, my soul waits, and in his word I put my hope' (Ps 130:3–5).

We often associate the strength and power of Simon Peter's ministry with the Resurrection, or Pentecost. He was a witness to Christ who was filled with the Spirit and preached with boldness. All that is true. But here Mark takes us down into the foundations of Peter's spiritual leadership. He was emptied first of all, that he might be filled; he was broken down, that he might be made strong; he wept, that he might know the joy of true forgiveness. Your experience will not be quite the same as his. But God has not discarded that pattern for moulding men and women into the Christians he wants them to be. Has he?

70

Suffered Under Pontius Pilate

Mark 15:1–15

One by one, all those who came into contact with Jesus reveal their moral inadequacies and failure. We have already seen the evil of the religious leaders come to a head in their plot to kill Jesus. We have watched Simon Peter's bravado collapse in the face of testing. It is now early in the morning. The Sanhedrin has found Jesus guilty of blasphemy (14:64). But its members knew that such a charge would not be recognised by a Roman court—and in their current political subservience, it required the condemnation of Roman as well as Jewish law if Jesus were to be put to death 'legally'.

We may well imagine that there were members of the Sanhedrin who were not present. Perhaps there were some members present who secretly felt great misgivings about the proceedings. But the fact of the matter was that all who were present consented to the verdict of guilty and to the fact that Jesus was 'worthy of death' (14:64). But further discussion was needed if his death was to take place. They would need to persuade Pilate—known to be a despiser of the Jews—to let them have their way. In the eyes of his enemies, the death of Jesus was not yet a certainty. It would need to be accomplished by careful political manoeuvring. And so it was.

Pontius Pilate

Our Lord was bound (v 1) and led to Pontius Pilate, a man whom history would have well-nigh forgotten were it not for his part in this drama. He was the Roman Governor. The power of life and death lay with him. This story gives us some insight into his character. He was shrewd enough to realise why Jesus had been brought to him; he saw through the envy of the priests (v 10). But he was too weak to do anything about it. When faced with the cries of the people: he 'wanted to satisfy the crowd' (v 15). Only Jesus stands with his dignity intact as he takes another step forward to his terrible, yet divinely ordained destiny. He is presented to us in this passage from three perspectives.

The king

Jesus is the king of the Jews who is rejected by them. He was accused by the priests of high treason. He had confessed to being the Messiah (14:62). His accusers 'translated' that for Pilate. It meant he had claimed to be a king. Anyone who professed to be 'king' was by definition rebelling against the Emperor, and was guilty of treason. This explains Pilate's question: 'Are you the king of the Jews?' (v 2). It also explains Jesus' answer, which is more fully given in John's Gospel (Jn 18:28–37). His words 'It is as you say' (v 2) are an affirmative answer, but they also display a certain reserve. Yes, Jesus is king, but he is not the kind of 'king' his accusers want Pilate to believe he is. His kingdom belongs to another world.

Pilate seems to have understood this. He did all he felt he reasonably could to have Jesus released. He did not see him as a threat to his own position or to that of the Emperor. What amazed him was that these Jews (whom he so despised) were determined to reject Jesus. It did not seem to make sense to him. What had Jesus done to make the religious leaders so envious of him? Why should they reject someone who claimed to be their king? Pilate must have realised there was something beyond human explanation in what was taking place before his very eyes. But, alas, he never clearly saw what it was.

THE SHEEP BEFORE THE SHEARERS

Jesus is also the sheep who is dumb before the shearers. As the chief priests hurled their accusations at the prisoner, he said nothing. He seemed to be resigned to receiving a death sentence. Pilate would not have known the Scriptures well enough to understand what was happening. But could no member of the Sanhedrin interpret Scripture clearly enough to see that the prophecy of the Suffering Servant was being fulfilled before them? Jesus was the One of whom Isaiah had spoken: 'He was oppressed and he was afflicted, yet he did not open his mouth; he was led like a lamb to the slaughter, and as a sheep before her shearers is silent, so he did not open his mouth' (Is 53:7). All the time Jesus was unveiling his true identity. But they did not have eyes to see it. Or, if they did see it, they were heaping guilt upon themselves moment by moment as they turned away from the clear revelation of the Messiah.

THE INNOCENT CONDEMNED

Supremely, in these verses, Jesus is the innocent One who is found guilty. Pilate was able to challenge the crowd's cry for Jesus' crucifixion with his question: 'What crime has he committed?' (v 14). The crowd had no answer. They knew he was innocent. Pilate knew he was innocent. Why then was he found guilty?

The answer lies in the interpretation of these events which Jesus had already given to his disciples. Why 'must' the Son of Man suffer (Mk 8:31)? It was, as Peter later explained, so that the just would die for the unjust, to bring us to God (1 Pet 3:18). He was innocent, but declared to be guilty. Another man (Barabbas) was guilty, but was treated as though innocent (vv 11–15). Jesus died in his place.

Without knowing it, the religious leaders and Pilate and Barabbas were all part of a tapestry of grace which God was weaving for sinners. Their actions spoke louder than their words, louder than the cries of the crowds for Jesus' blood. Jesus was not dying for his own crimes, but for the crimes of others; not for his own sins, but the sins of others. He did not die for himself, he died for us!

Have you ever seen what they were all too blind to notice?

71

Behold Your King!

Mark 15:16–32

Jesus had come to be the Messiah—the anointed prophet, king and priest of God's people. But throughout his public ministry his identity had been veiled. Conscious of how easily the claim to be Messiah would be misunderstood, Jesus had sought to inform his hearers what kind of Messiah he really was, before publicly acknowledging that this was his identity.

Now, however, he had confessed his Messianic character. He was 'The Christ, the Son of the Blessed One' (14:61). He publicly confronted Jews and Gentiles alike with his Messianic identity, and challenged them to respond. Only two responses were possible: acceptance or rejection. In Mark's account of Jesus' rejection he points out just how thoroughgoing this rejection was.

The prophet blindfolded

The religious leaders specifically rejected his claim to be the prophet of God, and derided him for it. They blindfolded him, struck him with their fists, and then mocked him, 'Prophesy! Go on, Messiah, tell us who hit you!' (14:65). We have to look twice at this statement and its context—yes, later, the temple guards took Jesus and beat him; but that was only after the Sanhedrin itself had shown its true colours and the perverted hearts of its members.

THE KING MOCKED

When Jesus was handed over to the secular authorities, his claim to be the Messiah was equally rejected, but this time the focus of the rejection is his claim to be king.

Having been cruelly flogged (a punishment so horrifying that many prisoners actually died), Jesus was now led away to be held by the Roman soldiers.

These men displayed one of the most frightening traits in the human personality: discipline of an unusual degree in one area, and gross moral indiscipline in another. They were neither the first nor the last to act in this fashion. But there is something singular about their little 'game'. They had called their fellow-soldiers together for an hour of entertainment with Jesus. Utterly alone, humiliated and virtually naked, Jesus was set in front of them in mock-regal dress—a crown of thorns and a purple robe. They called him 'king of the Jews' while spitting on him and striking him on the head. 'They mocked him' says Mark (v 20) until the time had come to lead him to the place where he would be crucified. They would show Jesus what they really thought of his claims. They did not have the eyes to see that the only thing they were doing was fulfilling to the letter the manifesto he had earlier published among his disciples (Mk 9:31). Even in the hour of his deepest humiliation, he was reigning as king.

Reigning in weakness

At this stage in the proceedings leading finally to crucifixion, a man might be too weakened to carry the beam of the cross on which he would be impaled. The soldiers therefore press-ganged a man by the name of Simon, from Cyrene, to carry the plank. Mark mentions his sons, Alexander and Rufus, which seems to indicate that they were known to the first readers of this Gospel—and if so had presumably become Christians. The story of their conversion was perhaps so well known that Mark did not need to say any more! If so, he could have given no clearer hint of the power of God's kingdom than this—in his weakest hour, Jesus began his reign of grace in one home and family!

The king must remain in control of all his faculties, and so Jesus refused the wine mixed with myrrh, given as a drug to relieve the terrible pain of crucifixion. Even now Messianic prophecies continued to be fulfilled: as the crowds watched, the soldiers cast lots for his clothing (Ps 22:18).

Earlier in the Gospel, Mark had recorded the request of James and John to be at his right hand and his left. They had not understood the cup he would drink and the baptism he would experience. Now two others were at his right hand and his left. These men, along with those who passed by and the religious leaders, poured similar contempt on him. They despised him as prophet ('You who are going to destroy the Temple and build it in three days...' v 29); they mocked him as king ('He saved others, he cannot save himself. If he is the king, let him prove it by coming down from the cross...' v 32). How blind they were to what was actually happening. Only if he refused to save himself could he save others. The very words they spoke could have brought them to the heart of the gospel. But they could not understand God's ways, or recognise his Messiah, even when above him stood the words: 'The king of the Jews' (v 26).

We are here present at a scene which Jesus must often have contemplated. As early as Mark 2:20, he had spoken of how he would be 'taken' from his disciples. As he had come nearer to that event he had explained its significance to the disciples: he would be rejected, would suffer and die in a cruel and humiliating fashion. None of this was unexpected; all of it was under his control. Crucified as king, he was king still. He made the cross his first throne.

72

The Priest Sacrificed

Mark 15:33–41

As the Messianic prophet, Jesus had been despised and abused; as the Messianic king, he had been mocked and enthroned on a Roman gibbet. Now Mark shows us that as the Messianic priest he became the sacrificial victim for the sins of his people.

As Jesus hung on the cross a strange darkness came over the land. Mark does not explain its significance to us. Perhaps he assumed that as his readers had followed the course of events they would make a connection between this darkness and the celebration of the Passover.

In the Exodus from Egypt, the plague of darkness had been God's last word to Pharaoh before the angel of death visited the land. Thereafter only those who were protected by the shed blood of the passover lamb would be delivered from the visitation of God's wrath. Now the Exodus was finding its ultimate fulfilment in the exodus which Jesus was accomplishing at Jerusalem (Lk 9:31). There was a plague of darkness preceding the sacrifice of Christ as the passover lamb (1 Cor 5:7). But this time, it was God's own firstborn who was to die.

Forsaken! Why?

This is why the terrible cry of dereliction issued from Christ's lips: 'My God, why have you forsaken me?' (v 34). He was experiencing what was involved in being the sin-bearer in the presence of the sinless God. As he came before God as the High Priest of his people, he carried no substitutionary sacrifice for them. He brought only himself. And thus as priest he also became the victim.

Mark notices several things about this dark experience.

Misunderstood

It was misunderstood by many of those who watched the crucifixion. They assumed that Jesus must be calling for Elijah. There seems to have been a popular religious belief in Palestine that Elijah acted as a kind of patron saint of sufferers. And so someone offered Jesus a drink—presumably in the hope of keeping him sufficiently alert to see what else he might say, or indeed what might happen. In the face of the most momentous event in their lives, indeed in human history, some of the crowd were incapable of understanding what was happening and what Jesus meant, because their minds were clouded with superstition. Had they known Scripture as well as they knew folk religion, their minds would have been drawn to Psalm 22. There they would have learned the true meaning of Jesus' death.

Symbolised

But the meaning of Jesus' experience was also symbolised by the tearing of the Temple curtain, from top to bottom. Mark does not specify whether this curtain was the one which stood between the Holy Place and the

Holy of Holies (Ex 26:31–5) or over the entrance to the Holy Place (Ex 26:37). But in either case the significance of the tear is the same: the old established priestly ritual for entrance into the presence of God had now been abolished. Jesus' death had created a new way into God's presence.

COMMUNICATED

Some element of the significance of Jesus' death was also communicated to the Roman centurion who was responsible for carrying out Pilate's orders. As he stood by, he heard something which was probably unique in his experience: a crucified man crying out with a loud voice, and dying (v 37).

Why was that so significant? Because crucified men often took two days or even longer to die. It was a death of prolonged agony and increasing weakness. Crucified men simply did not cry out with loud voices. They had no strength left to do so.

Exactly what the centurion meant by his words we do not really know. But Mark at least invites his readers to make his words their own. Throughout the Gospel, as we have seen, he brings us back time and again to face the question: who is Jesus? Here, in his weakness and rejection, Jesus is seen to be none other than the Son of God.

WITNESSED

Mark also tells us that Jesus' death was witnessed, from a distance, by the group of women who had ministered to him and the disciples in Galilee (vv 40–41), as well as by others. These same women reappear in Mark's narrative at Jesus' burial and then as witnesses of the empty tomb. They saw him die; they saw the tomb where he was laid (v 47) and they saw the stone rolled away on the first Easter morning.

Why should Mark include them here? Because they were eye witnesses of the central facts of the Christian gospel which were to be enshrined in the great creeds and hymns of the Christian church, as well as in the rest of the New Testament. Jesus 'suffered under Pontius Pilate, was crucified, dead and buried…on the third day he rose again from the dead'. The true priest had entered into the presence of God on our behalf, bearing the sacrifice for our sins—himself. Soon he would emerge, in full view of his people, his work completed, his sacrifice accepted, and communion with God restored!

73

The Grave of a Rich Man

Mark 15:42–47

Jesus was dead. Throughout his Gospel Mark has often described how people responded to Jesus at different stages in his ministry. He continues to do so here. In the lives of at least two men, the death of Christ confirmed attitudes which had been germinating in their hearts for some time.

It was mid-afternoon on the Friday of Passover week when Jesus died. Only a few hours remained before sundown and the traditional beginning of the Jewish Sabbath. If Jesus were to be buried, it would need to be hurriedly arranged.

Joseph of Arimathea

The body of an executed criminal was handed over to his family or friends only when special request was made to the Roman authorities. It is at this point that Joseph of Arimathea steps on to the stage of the Gospel history. We learn a great deal about him here. He was a rich man. He was also a man who had searched the Scriptures with a genuine longing for the coming of the kingdom of God (v 43). He had heard Jesus, and had believed in him, secretly, frightened of the possible consequences of open discipleship (see John 19:38). In his case, those consequences would have been considerable, because he was a member of the Sanhedrin—in fact Mark says he was a prominent member (v 43). For reasons we are not told, he had been absent from the meeting of the Sanhedrin which had condemned Jesus to death.

Perhaps that fatal decision of the Council had been the deciding factor for Joseph. Whatever else he understood about the death of Jesus, he knew he could no longer side silently with those who had so viciously sought his death. He must now come into the open. Even though Jesus was dead, Joseph was determined to follow and honour him in whatever way was left open to him. He came to the Roman Governor and asked for Jesus' body to be released so that he could make provision for its proper burial. Quickly he (and doubtless his servants) made the arrangements, and Jesus was buried in Joseph's rock tomb. A stone was rolled across the entrance, as Mary Magdalene and Mary, mother of Jesus watched (vv 46–7).

Crossroads

Joseph realised that no one can remain a secret disciple of Jesus indefinitely. There invariably comes a point at which we must burn our boats and cross our bridges. It may be when his real significance dawns on us with special power. It may be when others publicly reject Jesus, and we must confess that we will stand with him, whatever the cost. It may be both, as it seems to have been for this man. But in any event, every disciple must stand up to be counted. In the case of Joseph, he risked everything by doing so. We do not know what the actual repercussions were. We do know that 'it is with your heart that you believe and are justified, and it is with your mouth that you confess and are saved. As the Scripture says, "Everyone who trusts in him will never be put to shame"' (Rom 10:10–11).

Contrast

Joseph's boldness (v 43) is contrasted with Pilate's hesitation. Surely this interview was one of the great ironies of history. Here was the Roman governor who had had the privilege of interviewing Jesus, and on whose shoulders lay the responsibility for his life or death, humanly speaking—yet who, in his acting, was the instrument of God's purposes, all unknowingly. Here too was the respected member of the Sanhedrin which had voted the death sentence on Jesus. He was now an open disciple of the rejected and humiliated Nazarene. All Pilate could do was to confess his surprise that Jesus had died so quickly. He went through a formal investigation procedure, questioning the centurion in charge and then allowing Joseph to bury the body. It was tantamount to admitting that Jesus had never been a serious threat to the *Pax Romana* in the first place. Pilate knew that all too well. Yet his conscience seems already to have been deadened by the passage of time.

The one thing that really matters

The same twenty-four hours rendered the names of these two men immortal in human history. That is why Mark mentions them. But the one thing which gave both of their lives the ultimate significance they have was...what? It was their reaction to Jesus. Both of them seemed to think at one time that they could delay their final response to him, perhaps indefinitely. But events overtook them. The decision which Pilate faced 'What shall I do with the one you call the king of the Jews?' (Mk

15:12) was thrust upon them both when they least expected it.

It is often the same for us. We cannot pick and choose the timing of our decision to follow or to reject Jesus Christ, as though the issue could be delayed. God thrusts us into circumstances which confirm once and for all time the decisions and directions of our hearts.

As we come to the closing chapter of the Gospel it is time for us to ask ourselves: Where do I stand? With Pilate? Or with Joseph?

74

Resurrection!

Mark 16:1–8

Mark's account of the discovery of the Resurrection of Jesus bears all the characteristics of an authentic report. It is a psychological as well as a moral impossibility that the early church manufactured these verses. Several features of the narrative demonstrate this.

AUTHENTIC ACCOUNT

1. The women's role

Mark tells us that it was the women who first discovered the empty tomb and who heard the first announcement of the Resurrection. To our twentieth-century Western minds that may seem unremarkable. But in the context of first-century Palestine it was highly significant, for women were treated as second-class citizens. Their testimony would be inadmissable in a court of law. As witnesses they had no standing! No one who wanted to fabricate a convincing account of the Resurrection in first-century Palestine would have dreamed of doing it in this way.

2. *The story breathes authenticity*

In going to the tomb these women were following their hearts rather than their heads. Jesus had been dead for two days in a climate where bodies were subject to rapid decay. Further, these very women had seen the stone rolled across the grave. It was only as they walked together to the tomb that it seems to have dawned on them that they would be incapable of moving it themselves.

3. *They clearly did not expect a resurrection*

In spite of the fact that Jesus had told his disciples that he would rise again, the discovery alarmed them and filled them with fear (vv 5, 8).

As they arrived at the tomb, they encountered a figure in white—an angelic young man—who told them what had happened. Jesus had died as they knew. He had been buried, as they had seen. Now he was risen: they need only look in the tomb where he was buried. He was no longer there. He had risen!

True or false?

Since the days of the infant church men have tried to 'disprove' the Resurrection of Jesus. They have argued that the disciples stole the body, or the Jews stole the body, or Jesus did not really die on the cross and was resuscitated. But when we read the testimony of the Gospels, all of these arguments fall to the ground, and the testimony of this messenger remains. Had the disciples stolen the body, none of the marks of authentic reporting in this passage would be there. Nor would the marks of new power have been present in their own lives, had they known that the message they preached was pure fiction. Had the Jews stolen the body, the preaching of the early church would have quickly called forth his earthly remains. Pilate had carefully checked Jesus' death. But even if he had not done so, the idea of his resuscitation in the cool of the tomb remains ludicrous. For it involves the disciples preaching Christ as the truth but making the central element in their proclamation something they knew to be a lie.

...And Peter

Yet, while this defence of the historical fact of the Resurrection can be gleaned from the Gospels, we should notice that the burden of the message the women received was rather different. The disciples were to go to Galilee. There they would meet Jesus. And Peter in particular was to be given this message (v 7).

Why Peter? As we have seen, this was Peter's Gospel. But there is more to the message. This was Jesus' first word to his disciples since he had been torn from them in Gethsemane. His eyes had gazed on Peter's in the courtyard, but no words had passed between them (Lk 22:61). His Lord understood all that Peter must have been going through—the sense of shame and despair he had known as he wept bitterly. There were special reasons why Peter must meet with Jesus in Galilee. He needed to face up to his failure, be forgiven and restored to useful service. There, in Galilee, he would begin again to follow his Lord.

But perhaps the most interesting thing about these verses (with which Mark's Gospel probably originally ended) is their conclusion. The women were bewildered. They left the empty tomb trembling. They fled home silently, saying nothing to anyone they met, 'because they were afraid' (v 8).

Should they not have returned home rejoicing in the news they had heard? Is there not something unexpected about this response? That in itself is a mark of its authenticity (if we were to invent the story we would not end it in this way). But it is more. In Mark's Gospel, this fear is always man's response to the breaking in of the power of God. It is the fear the disciples experienced when Jesus stilled the storm; the fear of the Gerasenes when Jesus delivered Legion; the fear of the disciples as they saw Jesus setting his face to Jerusalem to die on the cross. This fear is the response of men and women to Jesus as he shows his power and majesty as the Son of God.

Mark began his Gospel by telling us who Jesus is. He wrote his Gospel to make us ask the question: Who is Jesus? and answer it accurately. Now he shows us the nature of a true response to Jesus. It is to be moved with a sense of awe and wonder that the Son of God came among men, and lived and died and rose again for our salvation. That sense of awe is the beginning of a new life of fellowship with a risen Lord.

Has Mark's Gospel brought us to know that, yet?

75

A Later Postscript

Mark 16:9–20

The Christian church does not possess the original manuscript of the Gospel which John Mark wrote. We have only copies. Sometimes those copies contain slight differences from one another. A word may be different, occasionally even an entire verse, as modern translations sometimes indicate. Here, in Mark 16:9–20, however, we encounter an unusual problem, as the *New International Version* text indicates. The oldest reliable manuscripts of Mark's Gospel do not contain these verses!

Handwritten Gospels

How could such differences occur? We need to remember that the Gospels were written long before the invention of printing. Mark was not able to take his manuscript along to the local printing press, ask them to typeset it, then read the proofs and have thousands of copies all exactly the same printed for distribution. If anyone wanted a 'Mark's Gospel' they had to sit down with what Mark had written and laboriously copy it out by hand. If, by any chance, they copied a word wrongly, or missed something out, then that mistake would probably be repeated when someone else took a copy of their copy of Mark!

When we remember that for fifteen hundred years people were copying the Gospel by hand, it is not surprising to learn that many small discrepancies crept into later manuscript copies.

How then can we be sure that we have the genuine text which Mark wrote? Only by trying to trace the copies back to their originals, by placing them in 'families' as experts do, and eventually locating the earliest copies of the Gospel and trying to work out, if mistakes were made in copying, where and how they took place.

A summary of other Gospels

It is not difficult to see how, for example, some verses might be added to Mark's Gospel. If someone had copied out the text, and realised that it had (as Mark's Gospel does) a rather sudden ending, they might well add an appendix, summarising some of the relevant teaching of the other Gospels, or the different traditions of the Church.

It seems likely that this happened in the case of Mark, since the two most reliable early manuscripts of the end of Mark's Gospel conclude at verse 8 with the words 'because they were afraid'. They do not include verses 9–20.

Of course, it is possible that the ending is missing in these manuscripts. Perhaps other manuscripts which are not so old are copies of even earlier manuscripts.

An addition

But most New Testament experts are convinced that Mark 16:9–20 did not belong to the original text of the Gospel. Why?

For one thing these verses are not written in the same style as the rest of the Gospel. For another, they read more like a summary of early church tradition than the material we have in the other Gospels. Their contents do not quite fit with the testimony of the four Gospels. For example Mark 16:12–13 seems to be a summary of Luke 24:13–34, but it does not really seem consistent with it. Again the promises given in Mark 16:17–18 read like a summary of some of the amazing things which took place in the early church. Nowhere else did Jesus seem to promise the kind of physical immunity which is spoken of here.

So, for these and other reasons (but especially because these verses do not seem to appear in our earliest copies of Mark's Gospel) it seems likely they are additional material which somehow crept in at a later date.

A STRANGE ENDING?

Why then does Mark's Gospel end on such a different note from the other Gospels?

It may be—as some have thought—that he was interrupted before he could finish his Gospel, or that the original ending of the Gospel has been lost. But these explanations seem unlikely. Certainly there is no hint in the records of the church that this is what happened.

The true answer is likely to be quite simply that Mark intended to finish his Gospel just as he did. He wanted to convey to his readers that the disciples (despite all that Jesus had taught them) had not expected the Resurrection. It was no piece of wish-fulfilment. They were stunned by it. And they were stunned by the implications of the Resurrection. Jesus really was the Son of God! He really would be with them for ever! They could scarcely take it in. Mark could not have expressed this more forcefully than he did.

The closing verses of Mark's Gospel leave us with some fundamental questions about Jesus and our relationship to him. That is exactly what the Gospel was intended to do!

Introducing Jesus

by Roy Clements

Large format paperback

People's lives fascinate us. Today more than ever we consume articles and watch chat shows, all to learn from a safe distance as much as we can about the joys and griefs of others.

Jesus had his admirers and onlookers too. But he remained a mystery to those who were not prepared to meet the man behind the image.

Through skilful exposition and challenging argument Roy Clements gives us an opportunity to get to know the real Jesus, as he takes us through a series of conversations and discourses reported in John's Gospel. He does not stop there, but goes on to relate the Bible's teaching to the beliefs and opinions of contemporary man. However you view the claims of Jesus, you will be left in no doubt that, correctly understood, they are of profound relevance to our lives even in this nuclear age.

'Some readers will surely be brought by the Holy Spirit to faith in Jesus. Others will have their faith clarified and strengthened. None of us can fail to be enriched.'

—From the Foreword by John Stott

'Brilliant, crisp, incisive and compelling.'

—Sir Fred Catherwood, MEP

'A book to set the soul on fire.'

—David Porter, writer and editor

Kingsway Publications

Knowing Jesus

by Gerald Bray

Large format paperback

Millions would claim to know something about Jesus. But what does it mean to know him personally?

This book takes us through the intimate portrait of Jesus found in John's Gospel, so that we gain a deeper appreciation of who Jesus is and what he has done. His teachings and miracles are explored in a straightforward and informal way that is especially suited to new Christians. As such it is an ideal aid to both private and devotional reading and group study.

Chosen for Good

by Peter Lewis, Roy Clements and Greg Haslam

Edited by Robert Horn

Three men, endowed with a remarkable gift of teaching, expound the basics of the Christian gospel. Here we see man in his need, in utter degradation and hopelessness. Yet we also see God in his glory, choosing to bring lost men and women back into the light of his presence and showering on them the blessings of eternal life.

In this book we learn—

— how God sees mankind today
— what he has decided to do about man's plight
— the meaning of Christ's death on the cross
— how we can believe the gospel
— how we can know God will never let us go

The authors guide us carefully through the theological minefield that has been laid around these great truths, and helpfully apply them to our everyday lives. As such it is ideal not only for new Christians, but for all those who wish to gain a deeper appreciation of what God has done for us in Christ.

Kingsway Publications